Acclaim For

Judaism: Ideas, People, and Rituals

Here is a collection of gems – each essay sparkles with knowledge and originality. Whether he's showing the Jewishness in Thoreau's thinking or tackling knotty questions about divine revelation, Rabbi Elkins approaches his subject with authority, clarity and utter honesty. Read and learn. This book opens up new worlds to explore.

Francine Klagsbrun, author of
Lioness: Golda Meir and the Nation of Israel

In Judaism: Ideas, People, and Rituals, Rabbi Dov Peretz Elkins demonstrates once again why he has been one of the greatest teachers and rabbis of our time. He has here culled together sermons and portraits of figures and movement to display and share his wisdom with us his readers and students. This work truly displays the knowledge, breadth, and insights of his learning that he shares so clearly and brilliantly. We are all the beneficiaries of his teachings!

Rabbi David Ellenson, Chancellor Emeritus,
Hebrew Union College-Jewish Institute of Religion

Here is a distillation of a lifetime of reflection, learning and encounter – real earned wisdom from a wise man. A book to turn to again and again.

Rabbi David Wolpe, Senior Rabbi, Sinai Temple, Los Angeles

Amongst rabbis, Dov Peretz Elkins has long been a legend. Upon entering the rabbinate, one of the first books I was told to buy was his book of sermons and essays, *A Tradition Reborn*. That was in 1973! Here it is in 2023 and I still turn to it for his insights and perspectives that are still relevant. He has the gift of bringing together the Jewish perspective on a variety of topics. How appropriate that his newest book bears the title, *"Judaism: Ideas, People, and Rituals."* Contained within it are messages and wisdom that relate to all of us ... every man and woman. The ancient religion is brought to life for the contemporary seeker. Who else but Dov Peretz Elkins could cover in one book subjects ranging from "human sexuality" to "hearing the sound of the Shofar". See how he does that, and much more! It's really brilliant!

Rabbi Mitchell Wohlberg, Beth Tfiloh, Baltimore

In this important collection of his writings, Rabbi Dov Peretz Elkins explores how Judaism offers us a path to meaning, purpose, belonging and blessing. He mines Jewish tradition, introduces influential teachers, and shares his own unique and powerful rabbinic voice. A must read!

Dr. Ron Wolfson, Fingerhut Professor of Education,
American Jewish University, author of Relational Judaism

In Rabbi Elkins's newest book, divided into those three areas of Jewish vision, relationship, and practice, the author treats us to some wonderful insights about all three, enabling all of his readers to understand why he is a committed Jew and thereby explaining to all of us why we might want to be too.

Elliot Dorff, Rabbi, PhD, Rector and
Distinguished Service Professor of Philosophy, American Jewish Univ.

Insights on Jewish Life

JUDAISM

Ideas, People, and Rituals

by Rabbi Dov Peretz Elkins

Winner of the National Jewish Book Award
and NY Times Best-Selling Author

Mazo Publishers

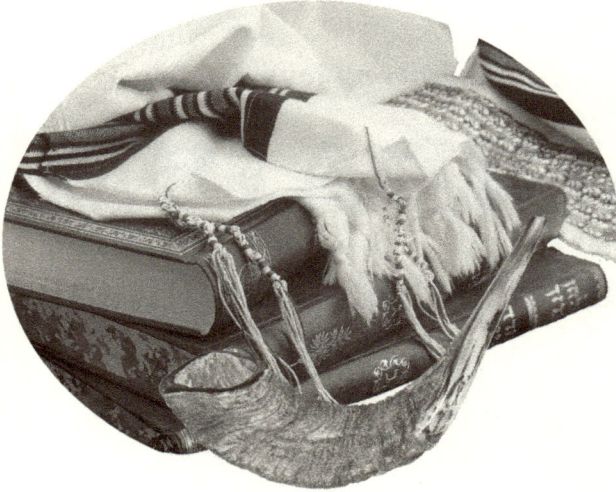

Judaism: Ideas, People, and Rituals

ISBN 978-1-956381474
Copyright © 2023 Dov Peretz Elkins

Contact the Author
RabbiElkins@gmail.com

Mazo Publishers
Website: www.mazopublishers.com
Email: mazopublishers@gmail.com

54321

In loving memory of my beloved family

My father, Edward Elkins
עוזר בן שרה ומרדכי הלוי

My mother, Bertha Sarah Byer Elkins
בתיה שרה בת חנה ויהודה לייב הלוי

My brother, Armin M. Elkins
אלחנן מרדכי בן בתיה שרה ועוזר הלוי

My nephew, Wayne Elkins
זאב בן עלא ואלחנן מרדכי הלוי

Turn it over, and again turn it over, for all is therein. And reflect on it; And become gray and old therein; And do not stir from it, for there is no better portion for you than this.

Pirke Avot 5:26

Someone's sitting in the shade today because someone planted a tree a long time ago.

Warren Buffett

Contents

The Author

Rabbi Dov Peretz Elkins is a nationally known lecturer, educator, workshop leader, author, and book critic. He is a popular speaker on the Jewish circuit.

Rabbi Elkins is a recipient of the National Jewish Book Award, and the author of over 61 books. His *Chicken Soup For The Jewish Soul* was on *The New York Times* bestseller list.

His most recent books are: *Rabbi Sabato Morais: Pioneer Sephardic Rabbi of Early American Judaism; The Battle Between The Menorah And The Magen David; Rabbi Alexander Goode: The Rabbi and His Three Fellow Chaplains Who Went Down with the USAT Dorchester; The Founder of Hasidism: Wisdom and Tales of the Baal Shem Tov; Peter Bergson – The Jewish Lobbyist Who Advocated To Save Jews During the Holocaust; The Friendship That Shaped Jewish History; Bialik: Israel's National Poet; The Power of Human Speech; FATE; Jewish Ethical Wisdom From Pirkei Avot; To Climb The Rungs – Memoirs of a Rabbi; Jewish Stories from Heaven and Earth: Inspiring Tales to Nourish the Heart and Soul; Tales of the Righteous, Simple Actions for Jews to Help Green the Planet; Heart and Scroll: Inspiring Stories from the Masters; In the Spirit: Insights for Spiritual Renewal in the 21st Century; For Those Left Behind: A Jewish Anthology of Comfort and Healing* and *A Treasury of Thoughts on Israel and Zionism.*

Among Rabbi Elkins's other books are *Rosh Hashanah Readings: Inspiration, Information and Contemplation, Yom Kippur Readings,* and *The Wisdom of Judaism: An Introduction to the Values of the Talmud.* See other books by Dov Peretz Elkins at www.jewishgrowth.org.

Rabbi Elkins served in several outstanding congregations in Rochester, NY, Cleveland, OH, and in Princeton, NJ, before retirement. He earned a doctorate in pastoral counseling in Rochester, NY.

Dr. Elkins lives in Jerusalem with his wife, Maxine (Miryam). They have six children and twelve grandchildren.

Acclaim For Rabbi Elkins's Previous Books

Rabbi Dov Peretz Elkins tells the heroic story of Peter Bergson (born Hillel Kook) who understood, before most, Nazi Germany's genocidal intentions, and devoted great efforts to mobilize the United States, in particular, to save European Jewry. Written in a manner accessible to young people and also of great interest to adults, Elkins reminds us that Germany's intentions were no secret, that American Jewry did not do enough to help, and that one man can make an extraordinary difference. Especially in light of the resigned cynicism that often meets claims of human rights violations today, the story of Peter Bergson is important to retell.

Dr. Jeffrey Herbst, President, American Jewish University

Peter Bergson (Hillel Kook) was among the first Jews in America to internalize the idea that the Germans were implementing the Final Solution to the Jewish Problem, murdering Jewish men, women and children throughout German-occupied Europe. He understood that this was not a time for business as usual and he raised a ruckus, pulling out all the stops to call attention to the plight of the Jews and to plead for their rescue. He organized, he publicized, he cajoled, he yelled, he planned, and he tried idea after idea.

History has vindicated his radicalism, his activism, and his boldness. Dov Peretz Elkins has made an important contribution in bringing Bergson to life, portraying him for a new generation, where he can become a model, an inspiration.

Dr. Michael Berenbaum, Professor of Jewish Studies
Director of Sigi Ziering Institute:
Exploring the Ethical and Religious Implications of the Holocaust.
American Jewish University, Los Angeles, CA

Dov Peretz Elkins has written an important book for young people. It is the heartbreaking story of a neglected Jewish hero, Peter Bergson (born Hillel Kook), and his desperate efforts to rally the United States government and people to make a significant attempt to save Jews from the Nazi "Final Solution" exterminations program which engulfed European Jewry.

The apathy of President Franklin D. Roosevelt and the Administration, and their unwillingness to act is vividly portrayed. The shocking indifference of mainstream American Jewish organizations and the callous policies of not rocking the boat pursued by Rabbi Stephen Wise are exposed. The spiteful attacks on Bergson and his various organizations and their allies by do-nothing organizations are ever more devastating to read.

Elkins describes the one success of all the rescue efforts – the appointment of a War Refugee Board which saved as many as 200,000 Jewish lives. One could argue that Elkins gives all the credit to Bergson and that Secretary of Treasury Morgenthau and his team's role is downplayed. But this would be nitpicking. All in all, this book is an important moral contribution. It pays a long overdue debt to Peter Bergson, to history and to memory. Tragically, it makes clear that human failures enabled the Nazis to operate with little resistance from America (as from the Allies and bystanders in Europe.) This book deserves a wide readership.

Rabbi Irving (Yitz) Greenberg
Dr. Greenberg served as Executive Director of the President's Commission on the Holocaust, which recommended the creation of the U.S. Holocaust Memorial Museum, and later as chairman of USHMM (2000-2002)

My family reads these stories out loud to each other. We laugh. We cry. A family that eats chicken soup together will remain culinary Jews. A family that reads *Chicken Soup for the Jewish Soul* together will remain part of an enduring tradition that has transformed the world with its humor, passion and generosity of spirit.

Alan M. Dershowitz, Felix Frankfurter Professor Emeritus of Law,
Harvard University Law School

Rabbi Elkins has written an engaging book, involving discussions among four rabbis of different religious movements. Through these conversations, readers gain insight into major – and minor – issues in Judaism. It's an opportunity for readers to "eavesdrop" on rabbis who are on the front lines of Jewish life ... to agree or disagree with them, to engage in their discussions.

Rabbi Marc D. Angel, Founder and Director of the Institute for Jewish Ideas
and Ideals and author of many books

In the Spirit is a lovely and accessible compendium of Jewish virtues that draws on our traditions of wisdom from the Bible to modern writers. Rabbi Elkins's own stories and comments make this book a valuable guide that can accompany the reader on many occasions.

David Ariel, PhD, former President of the Oxford Centre for Hebrew and Jewish Studies at the University of Oxford

Four Rabbis at Lunch is a marvelous discussion sprinkled with seriousness, humor and a great amount of important information about what rabbis have to deal with whatever their denomination and struggles. Much to learn from, to have a good laugh, and think about what Judaism is all about and why it is of crucial importance. The most important message of this book is that rabbis with very different ideas about Judaism can sit together, listen to each other and have an actual discussion. A hopeful sign!

Rabbi Dr. Nathan Lopes Cardozo, Jerusalem

Imagining, visualization, and meditation have been part of Jewish prayer and life for the longest time. In the Talmud we read that the early Hasidim would spend an hour before prayer in order to direct their minds to God. In his book on guided imagery, Dov Peretz Elkins helps the Jewish community recapture this grand tradition and practice. This guidebook will assist all who dare experience a new way of Jewish growth and development.

Rabbi Samuel K. Joseph, Ph.D., Professor of Jewish Education, Hebrew Union College – Jewish Institute of Religion

Few friendships in all of American Jewish history have been as impactful for Jews as the one between Eddie Jacobson and Harry S. Truman. Dov Peretz Elkins ably recounts the story of that friendship and what it meant for the emerging State of Israel. An inspiring story.

Jonathan D. Sarna, University Professor and Joseph H. and Belle R. Braun Professor of American Jewish History, Brandeis University

Since the 60s, I have cherished the books by Rabbi Elkins. He is generous and brave, traditional and cutting edge. He is a great teacher because he is a great student. Rabbi Elkins is a gifted Rabbi and teacher and writer. I always purchase his new books sight unseen, and I am always grateful for what he has written.

Arthur Kurzweil, author of On the Road with Rabbi Steinsaltz and From Generation to Generation: How to Trace Your Jewish Genealogy

Rabbi Dov Peretz Elkins is a leading spiritual figure in our time, and all his writings are of high quality.

Rabbi Zalman Schachter-Shalomi, author of Davening: A Guide to Meaningful Jewish Prayer

"What Rabbi Elkins does in this one volume window in the heart of the world's greatest Book [*The Bible's Top Fifty Ideas*] is truly amazing. His discussions are engaging, inspiring, comprehensive and scholarly. I have found his book to be exceptionally accurate, thorough and comprehensive. This is a veritable treasure. I cannot praise this wonderful book enough."

Professor Shalom Paul, former Chair, Dept. of Bible, the Hebrew University, Jerusalem

Through the lunch-table conversation of four imaginary rabbis, *Four Rabbis at Lunch* offers the reader an original perspective on the Jewish community and Jewish religious leadership in our time by a master rabbi drawing on his decades of experience in the Jewish community. The book's unprecedented fictional format provides the layman with a witty, anecdotal, and memorable entree into the complex, sometimes contradictory intellectual, moral, and social currents that lie behind the polished words of the preacher and the wise counsel of the pastor.

Raymond Scheindlin, Professor Emeritus, Jewish Theological Seminary

A most creative application of guided imagery techniques to Jewish education. If my Hebrew school teachers had used these tools to involve me personally and emotionally in my Jewish heritage, I would not have had to reach my thirties before coming to accept and prize my Jewishness. These activities are interesting, enjoyable, practical and useful with young people and adults.

Howard Kirschenbaum, co-author, Values Clarification

Dr. Elkins has compiled an exceptionally interesting and uplifting collection of essays and articles on the meaning and practice of the Jewish Sabbath. Readers of this book will be rewarded not just with new information, but with the kind of education that will help mold their character and forge their spiritual values.

Prof. Harold T. Shapiro, President, Princeton University

Rabbi Elkins has written another creative, useful, and user-friendly book that will help teachers, groups workers and Rabbis enrich their teaching of Jewish subject matter.

Audrey Friedman Marcus, Executive Vice-President, A.R.E. Publishing

What a treat! Dov Elkins has compiled a rich collection of guided imagery scripts, with invaluable suggestions for implementation.

Dr. Mel Silberman, Prof. of Organizational Development, Temple Univ.

Dov Peretz Elkins is one of the most spiritual people I know. His creative work in education and nourishing human beings is known throughout the world. He has made another useful contribution through this marvelous collection of spiritual quotations. His work continues to be chicken soup for my soul.

Jack Canfield, co-author, Chicken Soup For the Soul

"So, four rabbis walk into a deli..." Sounds like the beginning of a joke, but fortunately for us, it is actually the set up for a compelling peek behind the closed door of the rabbi's study. These thoughtful colleagues bring all sorts of fascinating questions to discuss with each other as they grapple with the key Jewish questions of our time: Jewish practice, intermarriage, fostering welcoming and inclusive communities, The rabbis may be fictional, but the brilliant Rabbi Dov Peretz Elkins is sharing truths stranger and more meaningful than fiction. If you've ever wondered how rabbis make decisions, grab this book. You'll find it hard to put down!

Dr. Ron Wolfson, Fingerhut Prof. of Education, American Jewish Univ.

This magnificent collection touches on the soul and secret of Jewish survival.

Sherwin B. Nulsand, MD, author of How We Die

"It's fun to learn the real meaning of Biblical texts. Rabbi Dov Peretz Elkins is a great teacher."

Edward I. Koch, former Mayor, New York City

"Dov Peretz Elkins is a gifted rabbi and teacher who has authored a number of books which are very popular among his colleagues. They will find this volume particularly appealing. It is a wonderful text."

Professor David L. Lieber, President Emeritus, University of Judaism

Preface

I was ordained as a rabbi at the Jewish Theological Seminary of America in 1964. From then until recent times I have taught, lectured and sermonized on a wealth of subjects.

The selection of the nineteen essays below is an attempt to put into one volume the themes that have engaged me deeply over the past sixty-plus years. Other themes to which I wanted to draw attention have turned into one of my sixty-plus books. Some of the essays have been strongly edited and updated. Others, I felt, were best presented in their original form. Those untouched are clearly ones that emerged from an early stage of my thoughts, and left as originally written or delivered.

The teaching of matters Jewish has been my life-long mission and my labor of love. As such, these essays along with my many book-length efforts, present a kaleidoscope of my yearning to share important ideas in Judaism and Jewish life with my students, colleagues and readers. May the Almighty accept this finite contribution of my life's expression of gratitude to my parents, my family, my teachers, my congregants and my students.

My devoted friend of our youth, scholar and mensch, Rabbi Stephen Chaim Listfield, has read the entire manuscript of this book, and most of my previous books, with a sharp eye and a wealth of information on many subjects, and has been an indispensable first reader, to whom I owe more than I can possibly say.

I also want to express thanks to my friend Hani Davis, who helped with editing several essays. My appreciation to my publisher, Chaim Mazo, who has brought to light many of my recent books, with great professional and artistic care. And special thanks to my loving wife, Miryam (Maxine) for her unfailing patience during the writing of all of my books.

Dov Peretz Elkins, Pesah, 5723, Jerusalem
The fifty-sixth anniversary of the reunification
of the Holy City of Jerusalem
The seventy-fifth anniversary
of the reborn State of Israel

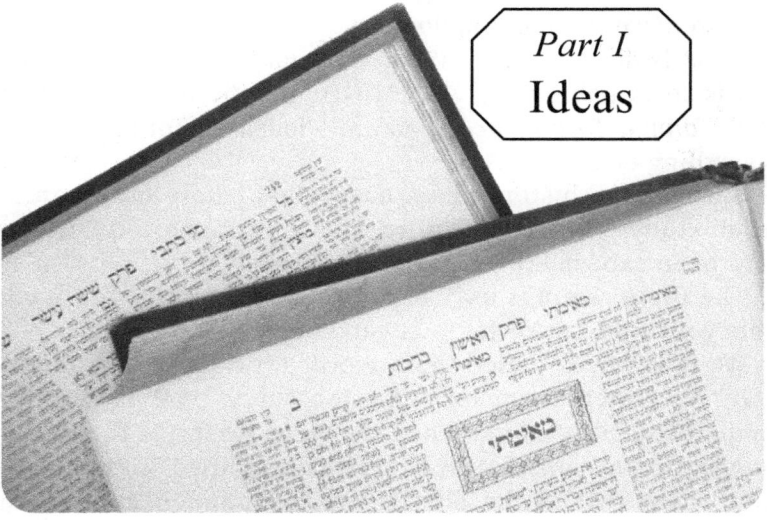

Part I
Ideas

| 1 |

The Importance of Jewish Learning

The greatest treasure that the Jewish People ever had is in your possession right now. It's worth millions ... it has outlasted armies and kingdoms.

What is this treasure? What is it that is right there with you that is so valuable? It's your MIND. It's the Jewish conviction that "*Talmud Torah k'neged kulam* – learning Torah is equal to everything else we do."

Throughout history Jews have given their best hours to Torah study – under all the various conditions to which Jews have been exposed through the centuries.[1]

The Bible reminds us "Let not this Book of the Torah cease from your lips, but recite it day and night."[2]

We Jews have studied those words for 3000 years, and have never forgotten them or neglected them. We have obeyed them. We have studied when we were weary at the end of a long, hard day's manual labor. We have studied Torah and read Torah books when the outside world hounded us and made our lives miserable and filled with terror. We would run to the *Bet HaMidrash* – the House of Study – no matter what the conditions, because – as the Talmud puts it – "*lekhakh notzarta!* – For this you were created".[3]

The measure of the success of our mind-oriented culture is evident in our presence here today. The most popular term we have for a Jewish house of worship is not "temple" or "synagogue," or "Jewish Center," but "*Schul*" – a school. We come here to learn. To be inspired, for sure, but our inspiration is more often than not a result of our study, our discussion, our library, our Religious School for children as well as adults.

The Hebrew poet-laureate of the 20th century, Hayim

---

(1) Louis Finkelstein – Introduction to *Lifelong Learning Among Jews* by Israel Goldman – from which much of this sermon was derived.
(2) Joshua 1:8.
(3) Avot 2:9.

Nahman Bialik, immortalized the House of Study – the Bet
Midrash – in these glowing lines:

Should You Wish To Know The Source

*Should you wish to know the Source,
From which your brothers drew...
Their strength of soul...
Their comfort, courage, patience, trust,
And iron might to bear their hardships
And suffer without end or measure?*

*And should you wish to see the Fort
Wherein your fathers refuge sought.
And all their sacred treasures hid,
The refuge that has still preserved
Your nation's soul intact and pure
And when despised, and scorned, and scoffed,
Their faith they did not shame?*

*And should you wish to see and know
Their Mother, faithful, loving, kind
Who ... sheltered them and shielded them.
And lulled them on her lap to sleep?*

*If you, my brother, know not
Then enter now the House of God,
The House of Study, old and gray,
Throughout the scorching summer days
Throughout the gloomy winter nights,
At morning midday or at eve...
And there you may still behold,
A group of Jews from the exile who bore the yoke of its burden
who forget their toil,
through a worn out page of the Talmud.*

*And then your heart shall guess the truth,
That you have touched the sacred ground
Of a great people's house of life.*

*And that your eyes do gaze upon
The treasure of a nation's soul.*

In William James's classic text, *The Varieties of Religious Experience*, the author talks about many varieties of worship employed by religions of the world. But one form of worship is omitted – it is peculiar to Judaism – study. The Jewish People made of study not only an intellectual activity but a religious experience. We have communed with God through poring over the holy books of our Tradition. When the great Temple was destroyed by the Romans in 70 C.E., we took our temple with us – our Torah – to all the countries of the world where we roamed, and were driven from century to century.

Perhaps the famous parable of Rabbi Akiva summarizes best the importance of study to the lifeblood of the Jewish People. When studying Torah was forbidden, on penalty of death, by the Roman Emperor Hadrian in the second century C.E., Akiva was asked why he continued to study, and defy the Emperor's mandate, thereby risking his life. He responded with this parable:

> *A fox walking along the banks of a river looked in pity at the agonized struggles of the fish in the water.*
>
> *"Why are you so restless?"*
>
> *They replied: "We fear the hooks and nets of the fishermen."*
>
> *"Then come on land, the fox advised.*
>
> *"You foolish fox," shouted the fish. "If we are not safe in the element in which we live, how much greater will be our peril out of it!"*
>
> *Our element, said Rabbi Akiva, is the Torah. ... If we forsake it, we destroy ourselves (Berakhot 61b).*

Love of Books

A sidelight of the love of learning, and clear evidence of its central position in the life of the pious Jew, was the love of the book. Listen to the words of Rabbi Yehudah ibn Tibbon,[4] who writes to his son, Shmuel:

---

(4)   12th century, Spain.

My son, Make your books your companions. Let your shelves be your pleasure-grounds and gardens. Bask in their paradise, gather their fruit, pluck their roses, take their spices and their myrrh. If your soul be satiate and weary, change from garden to garden, from furrow to furrow.... Then will your desire renew itself, and your soul be filled with delight.

The Nobel-prize winning Israeli author, Shmuel Yosef Agnon (1887-1970), wrote a Hebrew story, *"Bil'vav Yamim – In The Heart of the Seas,"* in which he tells of a certain rabbi who went on a hazardous journey by sea to Eretz Yisrael. When a fierce storm broke out, the rabbi was frightened, but when he saw someone sitting and reading a holy Jewish book, his fears vanished, because he knew "that no tempest at sea would cause him to sink and no beast of the deep could swallow him up." Agnon's literary symbolism was implying that the Jewish People will survive the brutal and wild storms of antisemitism, if they but hold fast to their books.

Hierarchy in Jewish Life

In some countries, it is political power that is the ideal of the masses. In others, it is wealth – or beauty, or art, or architecture, or philosophy, or *l'amour*, or gourmet cooking. Among Jews, it is learning. The elite of society was the Talmud student. Every Jewish parent wanted a scholar for their daughter to marry. The rabbis went so far as to say that a *mamzer* who is a scholar is to be considered above the Kohen Gadol – the High Priest – who is an ignoramus! What a clear statement of the hierarchy of values!

When we come to the end of our lives and are faced with the ultimate questions of accountability – how did we spend our precious short time here on earth, the most important question we are asked is: Did you study Torah?

I will never forget the orientation week at the Jewish Theological Seminary (JTS), when I was about to become a freshman at the world's leading institution of Jewish learning. The Seminary administration arranged for us to sit with Professor Mordecai M. Kaplan for an hour of dialog. When

Rabbi Dov Peretz Elkins (L) with Professor Mordecai M. Kaplan.

Rabbi Kaplan entered the room, we looked up at him in sheer amazement – knowing that we were in the presence of a giant in Jewish life. The person introducing Mordecai Kaplan was standing behind him, and motioned to us to stand. I later read of the law in the Shulhan Arukh, the 16th century Code of Jewish Law, that one must rise in the presence of a scholar. A few years later, when Prof. Louis Finkelstein was my teacher, several students and Rabbi Finkelstein approached the classroom door. Finkelstein waited at the door for one of the students to enter first. How surprised we were. It would be most inappropriate for a lowly student to enter before a great scholar. Then Rabbi Finkelstein explained: You are carrying a volume of the Talmud under your arm, he said to the student. The *Halakhah* demands that you enter the room first!

Prof. Louis Finkelstein.

I will also never forget one of the concepts Dr. Kaplan taught us during that hour. He said that the study of Torah is the education of the conscience as a life pursuit. A human being has an intellect and a conscience, he said. The education of the conscience is four thousand years behind the education of the intellect. Study of Torah, he insisted, is not only study of facts and information, but enhancement of our moral sensibility and sensitivity. We can ill afford to ignore that part of our soul. I want to return to this important idea before I conclude today's thoughts.

In other classes, during my five rich years at JTS, I learned that a school building was to be considered more holy than a Sanctuary where prayer was the primary function. The law is clear – one may sell a building for prayer to buy a school; or one may turn a *Bet Knesset* (a Sanctuary) into a *Bet Midrash* – a school. But not the reverse. One may not turn a school into a Sanctuary – because study precedes prayer in our value hierarchy. If one sells a Sefer Torah, the only thing that can be done with the revenue is to purchase another Sefer Torah. There is nothing more sacred than a Sefer Torah, and one may not descend in sanctity, only ascend – *"Ma-alin b'kodesh, v-lo moridin."*

In the year 1650 in the city of Gaya, there was an important session of the Moravian Council, which represented some twenty-five separate communities that met every three years to determine important policy matters. This council adopted a remarkable set of statutes that has come down in Jewish history as "The 311 Takkanot". *The First Seventeen Of These Takkanot Deal With The Study Of Torah.*

For example, every Jewish community with more than thirty families must maintain and support a rabbi, a yeshivah, and a minimum number of Torah students.

We in the greater Princeton area have two outstanding day schools, but it can take from 30 to 60 minutes for young children to ride there each way. If we lived under the rule of the Moravian Council, we would surely receive a hefty fine for violating a cardinal rule of Jewish life. We must consider the establishment of a Jewish Day School in our community, where our children can study two to four hours of Jewish studies each day, in addition to an outstanding program of secular studies and extracurricular activities. This should be the number one priority for our strategic planning committee in the coming years.

In the meantime, we must encourage more of our young families to choose the three-day option of Religious School for our children. Four hours a week is simply not enough to transmit a rich heritage that spans four thousand years. Our children are very busy with their secular studies, and we want them to succeed and excel in this area of their lives. But unless they know who they are as human beings, and as Jews, their true success in life is severely limited.

Emerson once said to Thoreau that Harvard offers courses in every branch of knowledge. Whereupon Thoreau replied – Yes, all the branches, but none of the roots. It's the roots that our kids learn here at The Jewish Center, not only the branches. This, in my humble view, is far more important!

We must also double and triple the number of children who participate in summer programs where study and Shabbat and Jewish observance is part of the daily schedule – places like Camp Ramah, the Young Judea camps, trips to Israel, and the like.

Our Havurah program at our schul should be strengthened and expanded, for many reasons, not the least of which is to have informal programs of Jewish discussion and study. Friday night in every home of our members should have on its schedule a formal Shabbat agenda of blessings, *kiddush, motzee, z'mirot, Birkat haMazon*, and not least of all a period of time to discuss the weekly Torah portion – the *Parshah* of the Week.

When I was a chaplain in the U.S. Army in the 1960s we took an eight-week course on how to be a military chaplain. One of the lecturers told us rabbis, priests and ministers that an army officer spends half his time in the military taking courses, in order to keep up with the latest developments in the field. Should not this also be the case with human beings – that we spend a major portion of our time keeping up with the development of our soul – our most prized possession?

I am not among those who look nostalgically on the life of the shtetl of the 18th and 19th centuries in Europe. I prize freedom,

*Chaplain Dov Peretz Elkins uses the top of a jeep
for a makeshift synagogue.*

democracy and autonomy too much to go backwards into history. But there are clearly elements of the life of our great-grandparents that has much to offer us. When Shakespeare put into the mouth of a Jew the statement that "Sufferance is the badge" of a Jew, he was wrong. He should have written that "Learning and education are the badge of the Jew."

A remarkable example of what I am talking about is a book located in the archives of YIVO in New York City that belonged to a special synagogue built by a group of woodchoppers in the city of Berdichev in the Ukraine. The book has a stamp on the inside cover that says: "Society for the Study of Mishnah of the Woodchoppers of Berditchev." That immensely impressive, humble stamp tells more than all the learned sociological treatises about the love of learning among our people. With a Jewish population of over 50,000, it boasted 70 houses of worship. And it had a large Jewish artisan class that maintained its own houses of worship, according to occupation. Who can be surprised, then, that there was a woodcutters' group populous enough to maintain its own synagogue. These people, among the lowest in the social and economic hierarchy of the community, formed an association – not for the recitation of the book of Psalms, which was a popular activity among pious Jews, not even for the study of the Parshah of the Week, but specifically for the study of the Mishnah, which requires considerable educational background and achievement.

I want to share with you the written record of the diary of a German intelligence officer stationed in Warsaw during World War I:

This diarist records that his office learned that something very mysterious was going on in the Jewish section. It was said that coachmen would come one after another without passengers and disappear mysteriously into a certain courtyard. The writer continues that he went to investigate for himself and arriving at the place in question with two detectives, stood and watched. It was true. Coachman after coachman was driving in with no passengers in his cab. All of them disappear into a courtyard into which the scholarly writer followed. He finally came into one of the upper stories of the building. There he opened the door and saw two long tables, surrounded by coachmen who were sitting in their high hats, bent over books, and listening attentively to a man who was expounding something.

The officer realized at once that there could be no question about a plot being fomented against the government. Nevertheless, he stood, dazed. He reports that he remained motionless, observing the occupants of the room without being able to comprehend what was going on. Finally he motioned to one of the listeners, for until then no one had even taken notice of the intruders.

Utilizing his imperfect knowledge of Yiddish, the officer asked the Jew, "What is this?"

"This is a synagogue," the Jew replied.

The officer repeated his question, "What is this?"

"They are sitting and studying the Law."

The officer asked, "Is today Yom Kippur, your holy day?"

"No," the Jew said. "This is what we do every day."

"You mean to say that every day you come here and listen to a lecture on the Law?"

"Yes, you are correct," the Jew said.

"After a hard day's work?"

"Yes, that is what we do."

The officer was convinced, and he concluded his account by saying, "It is amazing. It is unthinkable. It is inconceivable that German drivers should come every day to the University and listen to lectures on law!"

The officer, of course, could only have realized dimly, if at all, what the Torah had meant to the Jews through the ages; how, like a lone beacon, it alone had relieved some very gloomy pages of Jewish history, and how the Jew clung to it and found comfort in it.

I want to make sure to point out that I am not lauding the Jewish scholar today. I am talking about the importance of on-going Jewish education. Jewish knowledge is not only for academics, rabbis and Jewish professionals. It is the inheritance of the entire household of Israel. It is not how much you know, but the commitment to know more that is important.

The Talmud[5] relates a legend that at birth an angel puts his finger over our upper lip, and makes the dimple that we all have. The purpose of that is to erase all memory of the Torah which we learned in the womb. The point of the legend is that it is the value of learning which is supreme, and which is much more important than any knowledge we may have picked up along the way in our youth or since then.

So intent on stressing the importance of life-long Jewish learning, our Sages in the Talmud taught that if the Jews were to stop learning Torah, God forbid, for even a moment, the whole world would come to an end.[6]

There is a story I love to tell about a little girl who announced to her mother:

You know the beautiful vase on the parlor table which you said has been handed down from generation to generation?

"Yes," answered the mother, "what about it?"

"Well, this generation dropped it."

Surely it is not for us to drop the priceless heritage our ancestors bequeathed to us. As the Yiddish lullaby has it – *"Toirah iz de beste schoire* – Torah is the most valuable possession we as Jews own, more important than all our earthly goods."

(5) Niddah 30b.
(6) Shabbat 88a, Jeremiah 33:25.

Education of the Heart

The difference between study of Torah and study of general knowledge is that study of general culture enriches the mind and brings knowledge. Whereas Torah study adds to one's wisdom. As Rabbi Mordecai M. Kaplan taught at Rabbinical School, Jewish learning is education of the soul, of the conscience. It is designed to make us a better person, not a smarter scholar. It is designed to make us a better spouse, a better parent, a better business person, a better partner, a better friend – in short, a mensch.

Dennis Prager, the well-known Jewish writer and media personality, has a great line. He described some outlandish but "rational" idea, and says about it: "This idea is so stupid, only an intellectual could have thought of it."

Martin Heidegger, one of the twentieth century's greatest philosophers, was a Nazi. We know how many scientists and physicians used their knowledge to torture and pervert. No, it is not knowledge for its own sake that I am advocating, friends, but Torah knowledge. I am not promoting knowledge for its own sake, but Torah learning, for the growth of our soul. If Jews are truly to be what the prophet Isaiah asked of us three thousand years ago, to be a "light to the nations," we must be a people who act, function and perform on a higher ethical plane than other peoples and nations, to be teachers to the world.

That is what Torah knowledge can add to our existence.

I conclude with a favorite verse of mine from the biblical book of Mishle, Proverbs (4:8):

"*Sal-s'leha u-t'rom'meka* – Exalt her and she will elevate you." Or, as another translation has it: "Hug her, and she will exalt you."

When we return the Torah to the *Aron Kodesh*, the holy Ark, we sing, "The Torah is a Tree of Life to all who grasp her, and all who uphold her are blessed. Her ways are ways of pleasantness, and all her paths are peace."

Ken yehi ratzon – May it be Thy will!

AMEN!!

| 2 |

Is the Bible the Word of God?

The Problem

The very essence of the three great religions of the Western world is that God revealed His word to man. From their very inception, Judaism, Christianity, and Islam have held fast to the belief that their religion was not human-made, but God-made. The basis and authority of these religions was and is that God made His will known to His creatures through the sacred writings, the Bible.

When we ask the question, then, "Is the Bible the word of God?" we are questioning the fundamental principle of Western religion itself. If the answer is "No," then the authority of religion is undermined and in one bold stroke we disclaim the efficacy of Judaism, Christianity, Islam, and other faiths. This is the most serious question to which a religionist can address himself.[1] It is also significant because if we deny the authority of the Bible, i.e., that it is *not* the word of God, then we not only destroy the foundation of formalized religion but we undermine the authority of the values bequeathed to us from the Bible. Ethics and morality will no longer be able to point to divine authority for their sanction, and the structure of Western society as a modern civilization based on religious values will topple.

Indeed, this conundrum is no light matter and cannot be resolved in a comprehensive or exhaustive fashion in one short

---

(1) Julian Huxley (*Religion without Revelation,* [New York: New American Library, A Mentor Book, 1957]) and others claim that religion is possible without God revealing Himself to man. This religion, then, would not be Judaism, for in Judaism (as in Christianity and Islam) the thesis that revelation is the ultimate source and authority of religion still stands. All denominations of religious Judaism in America accept Divine Revelation, in whatever definition, including the liberal theological Reconstructionist movement. (See Mordecai M. Kaplan, *The Future of the American Jew,* [New York: Macmillan, 1949], 147.)

essay. By scratching the surface we will make an attempt to provide at least a partial or tentative answer.

At this point, the skeptic might say that the Bible is such a great work, or collection of works, that it can stand on its own authority. Whether the Bible is the word of God or not is irrelevant. The Bible is a great literary masterpiece. Who wrote it no more affects its literary qualities than it would the rhetorical grandeur of *Hamlet* or any other work of surpassing literary achievement. It would likewise not affect the historicity of most of the biblical accounts because these have been verified by historians, archaeologists, and Bible critics. The Bible as a monumental literary achievement and as an accurate source of ancient history needs no theological corroboration. But to Western persons the Bible is more than great literature and accurate history. It is a repository of ethical wisdom and moral insights that shapes our daily lives. If the authority of these values is cavalierly brushed aside, then the Bible would be just another Iliad or Aeneid, yet with the additional boon of being a source of Jewish history.

To quote an outstanding American rabbi:

> The chief value of the Bible is not in its literary power, its pervasive influence on Western culture, or its usefulness for Jewish self-comprehension. For the Bible has relevant things to say to the contemporary reader. Its profound insight into human behavior, its unfailing concern for human needs, its exacting morality, its insistence on a righteous social order, its vision of the reconciliation of mankind in brotherhood and peace, its tremendous intuitions about man, the world, and God, its sublime poems of worship and aspiration – all these speak to us with a force we cannot disregard.[2]

The Traditional Definition of Divine Revelation

Before we attempt to answer our central question, let us clarify what is traditionally meant by "the Bible is the word of God". What is meant when we say that God revealed Himself to

---

(2)   Bernard J. Bamberger, *The Bible: A Modern Jewish Approach,* (New York: B'nai B'rith Hillel Foundations, 1955), 84.

humans, i.e., what is Divine Revelation?

Our ancestors accepted three basic assumptions with regard to their belief in Divine Revelation:

(1) the Bible was written by the inspiration of God and is not merely a human literary creation;

(2) the Bible is the complete record of that revelation; and

(3) today we possess the full text of that revelation that was transmitted to our biblical ancestors – in other words, the Bible that was revealed to the prophets is verbatim of what we now have at our disposal.[3]

These three assumptions, comprising the traditional concept of Divine Revelation, were first enumerated by our ancestors, the rabbis of the talmudic period, and were later accepted by Christianity in both its Roman Catholic and Protestant versions. To this day, the matter arouses fierce debates among prominent theologians of each religion. The Roman Catholic Ecumenical Council recently dealt with the question in what is now known as its decree "On Divine Revelation."[4] It has always been a key question for Jews and Protestants as well.

But the source of the opinion that it was God Himself who revealed His will to the patriarchs and the prophets is in that record of revelation itself, the Holy Scriptures. In Exodus 19 and 20, we read about Moses ascending Mt. Sinai to receive the tablets of the Law from God. Further, and throughout the prophetic writings we encounter the phrase, "Thus saith the Lord." It was the rabbis, however, who expanded the doctrine of Divine Revelation to mean that Moses received not only the ten commandments on Mt. Sinai, but the whole Torah. They further believed that the Oral Torah, or rabbinic writings, was revealed to Moses at the same time. It is in the written Torah, however, that we have God's most significant and explicit revelation. For example, one passage in the Babylonian Talmud[5] claims that Moses even set down in writing the story of his own death

---

(3)　Cf. Moshe Greenberg ("The Study of Man: Biblical Criticism and Judaism," *Commentary* [March 1953]: 300–301), who phrases these assumptions in a slightly different fashion.

(4)　Cf. Augustin Cardinal Bea, *The Study of the Synoptic Gospels: New Approaches and Outlooks,* (New York: Harper and Row, 1965).

(5)　Bava Batra 15A.

in the last twelve verses of Deuteronomy. "Until this closing section, God spoke and Moses transcribed," say the rabbis. "When these verses were reached, God spoke and Moses wrote in tears." Another rabbinic sage held that Moses wrote all but the last twelve verses, which were recorded by his successor Joshua.

So strong was this belief in literal Divine Revelation that severe censure was prescribed for those skeptics who denied the doctrine. "Whoever denies the heavenly source of one verse or one letter in the Torah despises the word of the Lord".[6] In a passage in the Mishnah[7] we are told that whoever says that there is no *Torah min ha-shamayim* – Torah from a heavenly source – does not merit a share in the world to come. The rabbis took this fundamental belief very seriously and very literally. In number eight of his famous *Thirteen Articles of Faith*, the twelfth-century Jewish philosopher and codifier Maimonides writes: "I believe with complete faith that the entire Torah now in our possession is the same that was given to our teacher Moses, peace be unto him."

The Modern Attack on the Doctrine of Divine Revelation

With the advent of Rationalism in the last few centuries, many cherished notions of the past have been vigorously attacked. The doctrine of Divine Revelation was not immune to these assaults.

All three of the aforementioned assumptions supporting this doctrine were felled by the sword of human reason. The belief that God inspired the words of the prophets was no longer accepted. In fact, the Rationalists denied the possibility of God talking to or inspiring anyone. Toland and Bolingbroke stigmatized the Bible as a collection of inauthentic books. Morgan called the Pentateuch "a miserable system of superstition, blindness, and slavery; the Jewish priests deceivers, and the prophets the real originators of the civil wars and disasters that resulted in the doom of Israel and

(6)   Bavli Sanhedrin 99A.
(7)   Mishnah Sanhedrin 10:1.

Judah." Morton Enslin describes the attitude of one of the early attackers of biblical revelation:

> It was impossible to regard the Old Testament as a revelation of God, for the men therein [so say the Rationalists] depicted and praised are so unworthy that any fellowship with God would seriously compromise the Deity; the laws so barbarous and inhuman as to make their divine origin impossible; the miracles palpably absurd; Moses a disgraceful imposter, who by outrageous means made himself the despotic ruler of a free people and perpetrated in the name of God acts which would otherwise be on the level of highway robbery and inhuman slaughter; the spoiling of the Egyptians and the slaughter of the Canaanites tolerable only because of the word: "Jehovah hath said it."[8]

As scholars began to use the same rational criteria for evaluating the stories of the Bible, as they did for any other document, they found scratches and even breaches in the once-solid marble wall of ethical and moral principles. Such laws as that requiring the death penalty for a witch,[9] God's command to exterminate the Canaanites, or the prophet Elisha's curse that killed forty-two young children[10] exposed the Bible as a document devoid of moral value and ethical sensitivity. Moreover, scholars began to notice evidence of different styles of writing, inconsistencies between books, and contradictions within the same book within the structure of the Torah.[11] This further undermined the unity and integrity of the Bible in their

(8) Morton S. Enslin, "Biblical Criticism and Its Effects on Modern Civilization," in: *Five Essays on the Bible* (New York: American Council of Learned Societies, 1960), 35. The above-named rationalists are mentioned by Enslin.

(9) Exod 22:17.

(10) 2 Kings 2:23-24.

(11) Many of these were noticed by the ancient rabbis who, having accepted the above-named assumptions, could only whitewash these contradictions and inconsistencies through allegory and midrash. The boldest statement pointing to such matters was made by Ibn Ezra in his commentary on Deut 1:2; see Moshe Greenberg, "The Study of Man: Biblical Criticism and Judaism," *Commentary* [March, 1953]: 302–303.

eyes and proved false the assumption that the Torah was of one cloth, written by one prophet, Moses, and that the Bible as a whole was bound together by a single thread of content and authorship.

In addition to the new examination of the moral standards inherent in the Bible and the doubt of Mosaic authorship, there was a third reason for questioning Divine Revelation. The light of reason, according to the Rationalist mind, obviated the need for a supernatural source of ethical and moral principles. Reason, and reason alone, could act as our firm guide on life's problem-laden highway. No eternally "revealed" book or set of books was needed to lay down a set of authoritative and authoritarian norms. Authority was transferred from the supernatural to the natural, from heaven to earth, from God to humans.

In the words of Julian Huxley:

> Theistic religions usually adopt the hypothesis of revelation: they assert that the truth has been revealed in a set of God-given commandments, or a holy book, or divinely-inspired ordinances. The beliefs of theistic religions thus tend inevitably to be authoritarian, and also to be rigid and resistant to change. When change does occur, as is sometimes inevitable in our changing human world, it often involves merely the substitution of one authoritarianism for another, as when the Protestant reformers set up the authority of the Bible in place of that of the Church or the Pope.[12]

Thus, authoritarianism as a whole, whether biblical or otherwise, was rejected. The Bible could no longer serve as the source of moral, ethical, or ritual authority for the Rationalist. To Spinoza and others who followed him, the Bible had to be evaluated like any other book.

An Alternative Solution

Since trailblazers, by their very nature, are radical, the early Bible critics and Rationalist thinkers can be pardoned for any

---

(12)   Huxley *Religion without Revelation* (New York: New American Library, A Mentor Book, 1957), 185.

hyperbole in their destructive invasion of the solid house of traditional religious thought. Although many of the points advanced by these early scholars were valid and well taken, and are, in fact, accepted by religionists to this day, they made one error. They failed to separate the three assumptions mentioned earlier: that the Bible is Divine Revelation; that it is the total revelation of God; and that the form in which we now have it is the same as it has been for centuries via many prophets. In short, modern Jewish thinkers have divorced the first general assumption of the possibility, as well as of the fact of Divine Revelation, from the other, more specific assumptions linking this revelation with the whole Bible in a literal fashion.

Even though we can recognize strands of low moral standards in biblical passages, such as those mentioned above, this does not vitiate other noble standards of morality reached by prominent men in their time. Although the modernist does not accept all of the books of the Bible as a revelation of God's will, he nevertheless finds within it definite traces and signs of God's spirit intertwined in human affairs. Thus, instead of limiting the question of Divine Revelation to an all-or-nothing proposition, a third supposition suggests that the Bible is neither the total revelation of God's will nor is all of the Bible the revelation of God's will, but Divine Revelation *is* possible and has, in fact, taken place. Divine Revelation as a principle is accepted with new definitions, limitations, and expansions.

A New View of Divine Revelation Based on Tradition

The seeds of the modernist's view of Divine Revelation are not entirely of his own making. They, too, can be found in Jewish tradition. While we have abandoned one aspect of the traditional view, we now use another thread of tradition to formulate our new view, which can be considered traditional and thoroughly Jewish. It is neither a denial of tradition nor a rejection of the past, but a refined version of it. We are standing on the shoulders of giants and can thus see higher and farther than them.

The Human Element in Divine Revelation

The first insight into a modern definition of Divine Revelation is in the traditional Jewish conception of humans as God's partners in creation. As several modern Jewish thinkers have pointed out, Divine Revelation is not a one-way street wherein Moses or another prophet passively accepts the content of God's message, but, rather, it is a dialog between God and humans.[13]

Abraham Joshua Heschel has described the mutual flow that takes place during the Revelation of God's will to humans in the following words:

> "By insisting on the absolutely objective and supernatural nature of prophecy, dogmatic theology has disregarded the prophet's part in the prophetic act. Stressing revelation, it has ignored the response; isolating inspiration, it has lost sight of the human situation.... Careful analysis shows that this situation is composed of revelation and response, of receptivity and spontaneity, of event and experience."[14]

As Franz Rosenzweig pointed out, there are "three great moments in the history of the universe, when the divine decisively penetrates the world, in the acts of Creation, Revelation, and Redemption."[15] Humans, as God's partners in the world, have their own significant role to play in these three critical moments.

For example, let us examine the following rabbinic passage from Midrash Tanḥuma:[16]

> Tineus Rufus asked Rabbi Akiva: "Who makes more beautiful things, God or man?" Rabbi Akiva answered:

---

(13)   The works of Robert Gordis, mentioned in the notes below, are the source of much of what follows.

(14)   Abraham Joshua Heschel, *The Prophets* (New York: Harper and Row, 1962), xiii.

(15)   Quoted by Robert Gordis, "Revelation – God Speaks to Man," in: *A Faith for Moderns* (New York: Bloch, 1960), 150; Cf. also his "A Modern View of Revelation," in: *Judaism for the Modern Age,* (New York: Farrar, Straus, and Cudahy, 1955), 155.

(16)   Ed. Buber, Tazria, 7,1.

"Man makes more beautiful things".... He showed him ears of grain and cakes and said, "The ears of grain are God's work, the cakes are man's. You see that man's works are more beautiful." Then he brought them raw flax and some finished linen garments of Bet Shean. He said to him: "You see again that what humans create is more beautiful."

The same point is made in Midrash Genesis Rabbah 11, 6:

Whatever was created by God during the six days of Creation needs further improvement; for example, mustard needs sweetening, vetches need sweetening, wheat needs grinding, *even humans are subject to improvement* (italics mine – D.P.E.).[17]

What we see, then, is that Creation was not a one time event, but an ongoing process that is never totally completed. Our job on earth is thus seen as participation in the divine process of completing and perfecting the creation of the world by the Almighty. What religion has ever assigned a more noble and exalted role to humans on this earth?

As seen from the above midrashic quotations, a vital part of this ongoing process of Creation, in which humans are inextricably involved, is the spiritual perfection of humanity. When we read in the *siddur* (prayer book) that "God renews the work of Creation daily," we understand this to mean that every single day humans and God cooperate in the sublime venture of improving the physical and moral world. This is what Rosenzweig meant when he said that there are three events in which God's presence is especially felt – Creation, Revelation, and Redemption.

The doctrine of the human's exalted role in the universe is not a rabbinic innovation but an extension of a biblical principle. In Psalm 8:5-6 we read:

Thou hast made humans a little lower than the angels, and has crowned them with glory and honor. Thou hast made them to have dominion over the works of thy hands.

---

(17)   These two rabbinic passages were translated by Max Arzt, *Justice and Mercy: Commentary on the Liturgy of the New Year and the Day of Atonement* (New York: Holt, Rinehart and Winston, 1963), 65.

Thou hast put all things under their feet.

Unlike the theocentric New Testament, the Hebrew Bible is anthropocentric in outlook. Quoting Heschel, "The Bible is not a book about God; it is a book about man."[18]

The Talmudic commentator, Rabbenu Asher, writes:[19]

"For the Blessed Holy One is more desirous of mitzvot that are done to the satisfaction of human beings than those which are between humans and their Maker."[20]

Let us now take this thought one step further. So far we have shown that Judaism sees humans as God's partners in Creation, and that part of the ongoing process of Creation is the spiritual perfection of humans achieved through Divine Revelation. This does not make it any easier for the skeptic, who denies Revelation in the first place, to accept it. If we can define the process of the partnership more carefully, we will find a more palatable and inspiring conception of Divine Revelation for the modern mind.

In a striking passage in Midrash Exodus Rabbah 3:15, two rabbis disagree as to what Exodus 4:12 means when God says to Moses: "Now go [to Pharaoh] and I will be with you as you speak and will instruct you (*ve-horaytikha*) what to say." The disagreement revolves around the word "instruct." Rabbi Abbahu says that the word comes from the root *yara*, to shoot an arrow, and therefore God will supply Moses with the words to speak to Pharaoh as one who shoots an arrow, i.e., God will act as ventriloquist or ghostwriter and will supply Moses with a ready-made speech. The other view is that of Rabbi Simon, who maintains that the Hebrew word derives from the root *hara*, to bear a child, therefore God will make Moses into a new creature, give birth to a new Moses, i.e., God will remake Moses so that he himself will speak to Pharaoh; Moses will not have to rely on God for each word, but rather for inspiration and personal development to achieve the task himself. God will be the source of his remarks, but not the ventriloquist or ghostwriter.

The diverging interpretations offered by these two

---

(18)   Abraham Joshua Heschel, *Who Is Man?* (Redwood City, CA: Stanford University Press, 1965), 119.

(19)   Asher ben Yehiel, Germany 1250-1327.

(20)   Commentary to Tractate Peah 1:2.

rabbis from antiquity parallel the controversy between the traditionalists and the modernists. The former say that God was the source and ghostwrote the Torah so that Moses would act as God's intermediary and merely speak on God's behalf. The modernists, on the other hand, claim that the process of divine inspiration involves humans drawing upon God as the Ultimate Source of Creation and Knowledge that enabled *humans themselves* to speak and illuminate some of the dark pockets in the world. God's will is made known through Moses, who does not act as a passive vessel but takes the role of an active partner. It is a case of God and a human working together, a creative partnership.

To summarize, this one aspect of our new definition of Divine Revelation invokes a passage written by the modern Jewish thinker Ben Zion Bokser:

> The human and the divine commingle in all of life. The farmer tills the soil, plants, weeds, harvests, but this does not contradict a dimension of divine providence at work in the same process of bringing food from the earth. For the farmer did not create the earth with its power to fructify the seed placed in its womb, he did not create the economy of nature on which his labor depends, he did not stuff the sun with energy, nor fill the clouds with rain, nor did he fashion the seed with its miraculous power to reproduce itself. Throughout nature we witness what is a cardinal belief in Judaism, that man is God's partner in the work of creation.
>
> The partnership between God and man is similarly at work in bringing forth the truth on which our souls are nourished.[21]

Revelation as a Continuous Process

There is another facet of Divine Revelation adumbrated in Jewish tradition that makes this concept more palatable to the modern mind – that Revelation is not a one time event, but a continuous process. The implications of this view are

(21)   Ben Zion Bokser, *Judaism: Profile of a Faith* (New York: Alfred A. Knopf, 1963), 273.

enormous, and we shall explore them shortly.

The rabbis in the Jerusalem Talmud[22] recorded a remarkable point of view when they said: "Whatever a seasoned student was destined to teach before his master was already revealed to Moses on Sinai," i.e., whatever a contemporary scholar says in the mainstream of Jewish thought is Divine Revelation and an outgrowth or extension of God's original revelation to Moses on Mt. Sinai. It is a radical view compared to the more confining one that revelation ceased with the Bible.

Furthermore, the Babylonian sage Rabbi Yoḥanan stated:

> "God showed Moses the derivations in the Torah and the derivations of the scribes and whatever the scribes were to innovate in the future."[23]

Robert Gordis quotes this passage in a stimulating essay,[24] emphasizing the word "innovate" as a clearly defined statement that the scholar's own insights in the future will be derived from God. In other words, twentieth-century insights are also to be subsumed under the rubric of Divine Revelation. Gordis also points out that the idea of a "progressive and growing revelation is not merely compatible with faith in its divine origin, but is the only view that reckons with the [changing and evolving] nature of the human participant in the process.... the content of Revelation vouchsafed to men constitutes a growing and evolving body of truth."[25]

Revelation as Moral Creativity

Let us suppose that everything said until now is accepted, that Divine Revelation can be appraised anew as a creative partnership between God and man that takes place even in our own day, as it did throughout history, and that this view can be seen as an extension of traditionally Jewish ideas. Does this not reduce the Bible to a mere link in a long chain of Revelation beginning with Abraham and continuing with Moses, Isaiah,

(22)   Ḥagigah 1, 8, 76D.
(23)   Megillah 19B.
(24)   Gordis, "A Modern View of Revelation", 158–159.
(25)   Ibid., 156–157; see also: Bernard J. Bamberger, "Revelations of Torah after Sinai," *Hebrew Union College Annual* 16 (1941): 97–113.

Plato, Maimonides, Mozart, Freud, Einstein, and other creative people throughout history who have made significant contributions to perfecting the world? With this definition the Bible falls several rungs on the ladder of importance and authority simply because it is no longer unique.

Most emphatically not! While it is true that creative people are in large measure helping God draw back the curtain from the stage of a perfect universe, there is a significant difference between Divine Revelation as recorded in the Bible and other such revelations. I am not speaking now about the quality, intensity, or even frequency of the revelation (although these differ in the case of the Bible), but rather about the area of ultimate concern regarding the Revelation – the meaning of life itself.

Maimonides lists three prerequisites for achieving Divine Revelation:[26]

1. perfection in intellect,
2. excellence in moral qualities, and
3. a highly developed creative imagination.

Mozart, I am sure, possessed the first and the third, as did Freud, Einstein, and others. But Moses, Amos, Isaiah, and Micah, in addition to perfection in intellect and development of imagination, had an all-pervasive passion for excellence in moral qualities. Their ultimate concern was not one aspect of life, such as art, music, or science, but the totality of life and its meaning for humans and their view of the universe they inhabit.

The ultimate concern of the biblical prophets was the meaning of life and its implications for achieving the highest possible moral standards in living. In this area they were great innovators. In a world of paganism, superstition, primitivism, and human sacrifice, where human life was exploited and degraded, they achieved a new and daring conception of the nature of humanity as created in the image of God. In this field of moral living, they were the world's first and best creative leaders; their creativity was moral whereas that of the others was artistic or scientific.[27]

(26) *Guide to the Perplexed*, II, 36.
(27) Gordis, "A Modern View of Revelation", 155.

Thus, the process of Divine Revelation may be defined as *a continuous process of the human uncovering of moral law in the universe through a creative partnership with God.*

Living is a creative act. Uncovering truths of the world, be they artistic or scientific, are acts of great creativity, and since they uncover the inherent laws of the universe as created by God, these acts can be considered acts of revealing God's will. The highest level of creativity is that achieved by the prophets, later by the rabbis, and by such other chosen few who have made the refining of the moral order their ultimate passion and obsession, their very reason for living.

Since the Bible is the foundation of this evolving process of creative morality, we look upon the prophets as the founders of the chain of tradition we call Judaism. They sought out God's will in the sphere of ethics and morality, the relationship between humans and their neighbors, between humans and the universe, and between humans and their Maker. Not all of what the prophets said and did can be considered a revelation of God's will, but much of it was. For this reason, we look to them as the greatest of the world's moral leaders. We also look to their successors, the rabbis of the Talmudic era, for moral guidance and the unfurling of God's will.

Is the Bible the Word of God?

We now return to the main question of this essay and will give a concise answer. The answer is both yes and no. The command to exterminate the Canaanite population is clearly not the word of God; the laws of slavery, while more humane than anything then known, were only a partial attempt to reveal God's will; the command to love one's neighbor as oneself most certainly is God's will.

Why not merely attribute this great moral insight to human reason alone? Why must God enter into the picture at all? The belief in God is a matter of faith. For those who believe that God is the Creator of the universe, God is thus recognized as the source of all physical matter, energy, and creativity. One who believes in God recognizes that the scientist who discovers the laws of nature and invents new uses for known laws is revealing what God has created. One who believes in God recognizes that the world was created in harmony and unity, and giving purpose to our existence must likewise recognize that the prophet, teacher, or other leader who uncovers and formulates the laws of morality is revealing God's ultimate plan. Such a morally creative person has participated in a great divine-human adventure, which is the ongoing process of the creation of the world. The method by which one who has participated in this adventure can be called Divine Revelation. The Bible, as the record of uncovering many great moral laws and insights, can therefore be considered in large measure the word of God.

Since God is the source of all morality, when we say that Divine Revelation has taken place, we mean that some human being, through the perfection of the intellect, the highest possible development of moral sensitivity, and the development of the powers of imagination, has, in partnership with the Creator, revealed the will of God.

To deny God's share in the revelation process is to say that no partnership exists in creative morality, and that humans alone are endowed with the ability to discover moral truths without God's help. This would be the same as saying that humans not only invented the atom bomb, but created the atom as well. We would then have to change our blessing over bread as follows: "Blessed art thou, O human our Lord, king of the universe, who brings forth bread from the earth." For it is humans who, de facto, bring forth bread from the earth on the most mundane level: they grow the wheat, mill the flour, and bake the dough. Why not, then, say that it is humans, and not God, who "bring forth bread from the earth?"[28] We say that it is God who does it because God is the ultimate source of the bread – the earth, humans, the process of rain and evaporation, growth and life itself. To say that humans alone are the source of bread, or the source of morality, would be to dethrone God from God's central part in the religious person's *Weltanschauung*, and put humans in God's place. The implications and effects of this act would be to destroy the fundament of Western religion and morality.[29]

---

(28)   Cf. Shamai Kanter, "If Man Creates Life...," *National Jewish Monthly,* November, 1963.
(29)   Milton Steinberg, "If Man is God," in: *A Believing Jew: The Selected Writings of Milton Steinberg* (New York: Harcourt, Brace and Co., 1951), 306–309.

Maimonides's conception of Divine revelation was not far from the one just described. He says the following:[30]

"When we are told that God addressed the prophets and spoke to them, our minds are merely to receive a notion that there is a divine knowledge to which the prophets attain; we are to be impressed with the idea that the things which the prophets communicate to us are not altogether the products of their own conceptions and ideas. We must not suppose that in speaking, God employed voice or sound."

It was once said that with our understanding of the nature of the Bible, and the rejection of the second of the two assumptions mentioned above, namely that the Bible is *literally* the word of God, we no longer have *to believe* the Bible. Rather we now have come *to love* the Bible.[31] For Jews there is one further element. We must *study* the Bible, as did our ancestors through the ages. For they believed, as we must believe, that by studying the Bible creatively we steadily unfurl God's purpose for our being here on earth. In this act of Revelation we are *active*, and *not silent* partners. Through the study of the Bible we can apply the ancient wisdom of the prophets to the problems of our own day, and thus continue the long chain of tradition of a creative partnership between humans and God in making the world a better place. In this sense, then, we remember the wish of Moses,[32] "Would that all God's people were prophets."

With that revolutionary philosophy, we can well adhere to the idea of Prof. Moshe Greenberg, who was one of America's foremost Bible scholars:

It is in this deepest sense that we maintain the authority of the Bible. Not in the sense that its answers are final, or that it frees us from the necessity of the eternal quest and the unending spiritual struggle, but in the sense that the ultimate answers, when attained, will be found at the end of a road that

(30)   Bokser, *Judaism: Profile of a Faith*, 267. (*Guide To the Perplexed*, I, 65).

(31)   Enslin, "Biblical Criticism and Its Effects on Modern Civilization," in: *Five Essays on the Bible* (New York: American Council of Learned Societies, 1960), 44.

(32)   Numbers 11:29.

is drawn in the Bible as if on a map.[33]

Further Reading:

Bamberger, Bernard J., *The Bible: A Modern Jewish Approach* (New York: B'nai B'rith Hillel Foundations, 1955).

Enslin, Morton S., "Biblical Criticism and Its Effects on Modern Civilization," in: *Five Essays on the Bible* (New York: American Council of Learned Societies, 1960), 30–44.

Gordis, Robert, "A Modern View of Revelation," in: *Judaism for the Modern Age* (New York: Farrar, Straus, and Cudahy, 1955), 153–165.

– – – , "Revelation – God Speaks to Man," in: *A Faith for Moderns* (New York: Bloch, 1960), 136–155.

– – – , "The Bible for Moderns," in: *Jewish Heritage Reader*, ed. Lily Edelman (New York: Taplinger Publishing, 1965), 345–350.

Greenberg, Moshe, "The Study of Man: Biblical Criticism and Judaism," *Commentary* (March, 1953): 298–304.

Heschel, Abraham J., *The Prophets* (New York: Harper and Row, 1962), Chapters 22–26.

Tillich, Paul, "The Truth of Faith," in: *Dynamics of Faith* (New York: Harper and Row, 1957), 74–98.

---

(33)   Greenberg, "The Study of Man: Biblical Criticism and Judaism," *Commentary,* March 1953, 303.

| 3 |

How Judaism Encourages Self-Esteem

I wrote my doctoral dissertation at Colgate Rochester Divinity School in 1976, on self-esteem, under the direction of a wonderful professor, Edward Thornton. I created a manual titled *Teaching People to Love Themselves*. Developed into book form, it has been one of my best-selling books, next to *Chicken Soup for the Jewish Soul*. In the 1960s and 1970s, self-esteem was a major theme in the Human Potential Movement. I was inspired to delve into this subject after enrolling in a week-long workshop led by Jack Canfield. Following that workshop, Jack and I led self-esteem workshops in several cities throughout the USA, and Jack and I became good friends. Some time later Jack, who initiated the Chicken Soup for the Soul series (now up to almost three hundred titles, and sold well over a million copies). The book I co-edited, on the "Jewish Soul" has sold about 200,000 copies. Obviously the theme of self-esteem has been a significant topic for many, including for Jews.

What are the results which people hope to achieve in working to develop self-esteem?

Expert psychologists in the field teach that self-esteem is a key ingredient in human behavior. It is both the product and producer of experience. If an individual thinks s/he can do something it is likely that s/he can do it. It is a self-fulfilling prophecy. Self-esteem is also a major factor in creating healthy relationships.

Consider the following allegory:[1]

> A mouse ran into the office of the Educational Testing Service and accidentally triggered a delicate point in the apparatus just as the College Entrance Examination Board's data on one Henry Carson was being scored.
>
> Henry was an average high-school student who was unsure of himself and his abilities. Had it not been for

---

[1]   William W. Purkey, included in *Glad to Be Me*, ed. Dov Peretz Elkins, Revised Edition, 1989, p. 89.

the mouse, Henry's scores would have been average or less, but the mouse changed all that, for the scores which emerged from the computer were amazing-800's in both the verbal and quantitative areas.

When the scores reached Henry's school, the word of his giftedness spread like wildfire. Teachers began to reevaluate their gross underestimation of this fine lad, counselors trembled at the thought of neglecting such talent, and even college admissions officers began to recruit Henry for their schools.

New worlds opened for Henry, and as they opened he started to grow as a person and as a student. Once he became aware of his potential and began to be treated differently by the significant people in his life, a form of self-fulfilling prophecy took place. Henry gained in confidence and began "to put his mind in the way of great things." ... Henry became one of the best men of his generation.

One of the conventional assumptions about loving self and others is that love is quantifiable. That is, if you give love to someone, you are giving it away, and you have less to share with others or self. This is obviously erroneous. The more love we give, the more we are likely to have to give and receive, for others and self.

Another erroneous assumption is that narcissism is bestowing too much love on yourself. In reality, a narcissist is one who has low self-esteem, and thinks that by being selfish one can acquire more love for self. A person with strong self-esteem is less likely to become narcissistic.

Jewish Sources on Self-Esteem

The Jewish tradition long ago understood that loving oneself is an important component of a healthy personality.

Many passages in rabbinic literature conspire to promote high self-esteem. An important Talmudic principle is *"Adam karov aytzel atzmo – a person is close to oneself."* This Talmudic idea means that a person is not trustworthy to testify [in court] about himself, for his own benefit or even to his detriment.

Sometimes a story illustrates a legal principle better than a declarative statement. Let's look at one Talmudic tale about the famous Rabbi Akiva and another Talmudic colleague, named Ben Petura.[2]

It was taught: two walking in the desert with only a canteen of water between them. If they both drink then both will die [i.e. there is not enough water to sustain both of them]. Yet if one of them drinks he will survive long enough to return to a settlement. Ben Petura expounded, better for both to drink and die rather than for one to see the death of his friend. Until Rabbi Akiva arrived and taught "Your brother shall live with you[3] your brother may live" i.e., your life must come first.

In teaching this Talmudic passage, I frequently use the example of the rules of seatbelts on an airplane. The flight attendant announces that if one is flying with a child, it is important to fasten one's own seatbelt first, and only then help the child with his/her seatbelt. The assumption on an airplane is the same assumption in the story of Rabbi Akiva and Ben Petura, namely, that caring for oneself is a prerequisite for helping others. Self-care, or self-esteem, is the necessary ingredient to be helpful to others.

Loving oneself, caring for oneself, was an important theme among Hasidic teachers in the eighteenth and nineteenth centuries.

One Hasidic master, the Maggid of Mezerich[4] taught that there are times when humility must be replaced by immodesty. He based his teaching on an ancient teaching[5] that "Torah clothes one in humility." (That is, genuine study of Torah should make you humble, not proud of your learning). Says the Maggid, if humility is a cloak, then one can take it off, and not be modest in a situation where modesty is not called for. That is, a case where one should sometimes discard the quality of modesty when active self-care is called for.

---

(2)   Bava Metzia, 62A.
(3)   Leviticus 25:36.
(4)   1704-1772, Poland.
(5)   Pikei Avot 6:1.

Another story from the Hasidic tradition illustrates a similar point. This is about the famous Rabbi Zusha of Arnipol.[6] When Rabbi Zusha was on his deathbed, his students found him in uncontrollable tears. They tried to comfort him by telling him that he was almost as wise as Moses and as kind as Abraham, so he was sure to be judged positively in Heaven. He replied, "When I get to Heaven, I will not be asked Why weren't you like Moses, or Why weren't you like Abraham. They will ask, Why weren't you like Zusha?" Why didn't he fully live up to his own potential? The lesson is that one can love who you are, and not try to be someone else.

A profound teaching was offered to Jews in Eastern Europe during times of persecution. Rabbis would tell their followers that they should not think of themselves as unworthy, just because evil people treat them unfairly. They should rather think of themselves in a positive way. "*Bei dem Ribono shel olam bis du a kenig* – In the eyes of the Creator of the Universe, you are royalty."

The thrust of Jack Canfield's teaching, in his workshops and in his widely read book, *101 Ways to Develop Student Self-Esteem*, is to affirm and compliment others, and to be careful of words that can be considered "put-downs." Too often we wait until someone's funeral to offer praise about them.

Professor Dale Baum of Texas A&M University tells this adorable anecdote about the importance even little children place on receiving praise:

> Every person needs recognition. It is expressed cogently by the child who says: "Mother, let's play darts. I'll throw the darts, and you say 'Wonderful.'"

Howard Clinebell, a professor of pastoral counseling, wrote that "without a solid sense of self-worth, a person is limited in his ability to live fully, to relate in a mutually fulfilling way, and to find a religious life in real depth."

There is a wonderful Hebrew phrase used often in synagogue, given to a person who has any number of honors during worship – such as having an honor at the Torah, leading a prayer, or chanting words from the Torah. The phrase is "*yishar koah,*" or "may your strength be increased." This phrase

(6)   1718-1800, Ukraine.

is used regardless of whether the honoree did a magnificent job in his chanting or reading, or even if it was just ordinary. The custom encourages each person to offer praise to others. We all need such praise, and receiving a *"yishar koah"* is always greatly appreciated.

Groups as well as individuals need to have self-esteem, need to have the group – ethnic, racial, national, religious, or whatever.

Phrases such as "black is beautiful" helped many African Americans beginning in the 1960s to overcome feelings of inferiority. It aimed to dispel the racist notion that black people's natural features such as skin color, facial features and hair are inherently ugly. The phrase "black is beautiful" encompassed emotional and psychological well-being of black people. It promoted black culture and identity, so that the black past was an inspirational cultural pride. It affirmed the beauty of Blacks' natural features, such as their variety of skin colors, hair styles and textures, as well as affirming black culture in literature and the arts.

In similar fashion, many Jews have needed an affirmation of their ethnic and religious identity because of the omnipresent disease of antisemitism. The stereotypical self-loathing Jew might dismiss an antisemitic joke as good-humor, but consider it in poor taste to tell a humorous story about a non-Jewish clergyperson.

There is an anecdote about a Jew who was embarrassed at seeing a fellow Jew in Hasidic garb, but when viewing a person with similar clothing on an Amish individual would consider it quaint. Similarly, a Jew without good self-esteem regarding one's faith tradition might be embarrassed to carry a *tallit* – prayer shawl – and hide it in a paper bag, but when seeing a Christian carrying a frond on Palm Sunday would consider it admirable. Or consider a Jew who thinks relatives at a bar mitzvah or wedding reception are loud and vulgar, but reflects on Italians at a wedding party as happily picturesque.

The ancient rabbis often encouraged a sense of pride in oneself, and a healthy dose of self-esteem in one's ethnic and religious heritage. The *midrash,* ancient rabbinic biblical commentary, claims that one of the reasons the biblical

Hebrews were redeemed from Egypt is because they entered Egypt as Reuven and Shimon, and left as Reuven and Shimon, and did not alter their names by calling Reuven Rufus, and Judah as Julian, or Joseph as Luke.[7]

In other words, the virtue of self-pride in not assimilating into foreign culture, but maintaining their true identity, was meritorious, and made them worthy of redemption.

A traditional Jew recites these wholesome words each morning in the daily liturgy: "How goodly is our portion, how pleasant our lot, how beautiful our heritage."

Though Albert Einstein was not a ritually observant Jew, he took great pride in his being a Jew. Among his many statements of pride in being Jewish, this one stands out:

> Before we can effectively combat antisemitism, we must first of all educate ourselves out of it, and out of the slave-mentality which it betokens. Only when we respect ourselves, can we win the respect of others; or rather, the respect of others will then come of itself.

Other proud Jews have made important statements about the importance of accepting themselves, and loving their ethnic/religious status of being Jewish, as opposed to trying to assimilate into the general culture surrounding them.

Let's start with a beautiful statement of Jewish self-pride, self-acceptance, and self-esteem by the Nobel Prize winning Holocaust survivor and world-class writer, Elie Wiesel:

> Remember: the Jew influences his environment only if he does not assimilate. Others will benefit from his experience to the degree that it is and remains unique. Only by assuming his Jewishness can he attain universality. The Jew who repudiates himself, claiming to do so for the sake of humanity, will inevitably repudiate humanity too. A lie cannot be a stepping stone to truth: it can only be an obstacle.... By working for his own people a Jew does not renounce his loyalty to mankind. On the contrary, he makes his most valuable contribution.... By struggling on behalf of Russian, Arab, or Polish Jews, I fight for human rights everywhere. By calling for peace in

---

(7) Vayikra (Leviticus) Rabbah, chapter 32:5.

the Middle East, I take a stand against every aggression, every war. By protesting the fanatical exhortations to "holy wars" against my people, I protest against the stifling of freedom in Prague. By striving to keep alive the memory of the Holocaust, I denounce the massacres in Biafra and the nuclear menace. Only by drawing on his unique experience can the Jew help others. A Jew fulfills his role as man only from inside his Jewishness.

A clever parable by the late Rabbi Saul Teplitz makes the same point in an indirect, but clear message:

"There was once a scottie dog who found himself lost and alone in a neighborhood of Irish terriers. Every time the scottie walked down the street, the terriers would bark at him in rage. He was quite puzzled and hurt, but instead of wondering what bothered the terriers, he began to analyze himself. Perhaps the terriers barked at him because he was different. He, therefore, tried very hard to be like the terriers. He began to wag his tail as they did and to prick up his ears as they did. He even barked in as perfect an imitation as could be achieved. And still they barked every time he went by.

"The scottie then decided to call in experts to write scholarly dissertations which would prove the greatness of the contributions of the scotties to canine civilization. Soon there were mountains of statistics to point up the courage of the scotties, through a computation of the number of people they had rescued from burning buildings and drownings. Unfortunately, the only ones that read the books and the statistics were other scotties.

"Whatever the scottie did to impress or to imitate left the terriers unmoved. They continued to bark as in the past. Finally, the scottie decided that since he was a scottie, he had better act like one and live like one, and be the best possible scottie he could be. And if the terriers still barked, there was nothing he could do about it."

The founder of Hasidism, Israel Baal Shem Tov[8] framed his message in these words:

---

(8)   1700-1760, Ukraine.

What is the interpretation of the biblical command, "Thou shalt love thy neighbor as thyself?" What does it mean to love our neighbor as we love ourselves?

The Baal Shem explained:

How does one love himself? A person does not look for reasons to love himself. Man does not say: "I am nice. I am smart. I am generous, therefore I am deserving of my love." No. We love ourselves knowing our weaknesses, our shortcomings, our meanness, our vices. In the same manner we are to love our fellow men. To love for a reason is to love the reason, not the person. The reason departs, the love with it. True love is love without a reason.

Finally, we sum up the message of this essay with the words of the sainted Rabbi Menahem Mendel of Vitebsk:[9]

Rejoice that you have an opportunity to sing unto God.
Rejoice that you are a Jew.
Rejoice that you are able to pray, to study and
        to perform God's will.
Before the endlessness of God, the highest saint
        and the lowliest commoner are equal.
Be contented with your achievements in affairs of the spirit,
        as well as with your worldly status.
Do not doubt yourself, but enjoy the Light of God.

(9)   1730-1788, Belarus.

| 4 |

How to Raise a Jewish Child to be Jewish and a Mensch

An ancient midrash[1] illustrates the importance that Jewish tradition gives to the importance of children.

Rabbi Meir taught:

When the Israelites came to receive the Torah, God said to them: "Bring to Me good sureties that you will observe it."

They answered: "Our Patriarchs will be our sureties."

God answered: "Your sureties need sureties themselves. I have found fault with them."

They answered: "Our Prophets will be our sureties."

God replied "I have found fault with them also."

Then the Israelites said; "Our children will be our sureties."

They proved acceptable, and God gave to Israel the Torah.

There are several humorous tales that also testify to the central concern Jews have for their children.

Three Jewish women meet weekly for a game of cards and refreshments. The first woman says: Oy! The second woman likewise says: Oy! The third woman reacts: "I thought we were not going to talk about the children today."

Then there are proverbs that also testify to this unrelenting concern for the welfare of children.

A Jewish father tells a Russian-Jewish immigrant:

"In America we have a proverb: Little children, little problems; big children, big problems."

(1)   Shir HaShirim Rabbah, on verse 1:4.

The immigrant responded:

"In Russia we used to say: Little children don't let you sleep; big children don't let you live."

Then there is an Oriental proverb, with a slightly different slant:

"Your child at age five is your master; at age ten, your slave; at fifteen, your double. After that, your friend or foe, depending on his or her upbringing."

Five Rules

I hesitate to offer rules for child-rearing. This anecdote will explain why.

A young psychologist advertised a lecture he was available to deliver, "*Twelve Rules for Raising Children.*"

After his wife gave birth to their first child, he changed the title of his lecture to "*Twelve Suggestions for Raising Children.*"

After his family grew, and there were three children, he again changed the title of his lecture to "*Twelve Hints for Raising Children.*"

So the following are not exactly "rules," but perhaps suggestions or hints.

The first "rule" is that children, like adults, need love and respect. Receiving love and respect helps to raise a child's self-esteem.

The German poet Johann von Goethe (1749-1832), in his epic poem, "Hermann and Dorothea," puts these words into the mouth of the wise mother:

"We have no power to fashion our children as suits our fancy; As they are given by God, so must we have them and love them. Teach them as best we can, and let each of them follow his nature."

Erma Bombeck (1927-1996), the well-known author of a humorous newspaper column, demonstrated the need to respect children in this column: "Treat Kids the Same as Friends." ... On TV the other day, a leading child psychologist said parents should treat their children as they would treat their best friend ... with courtesy, dignity and diplomacy.

"I have never treated my children any other way," I told myself. But later that night, I thought about it. Did I really talk to my best friends like I talked to my children? Just suppose ... our good friends, Fred and Eleanor, came to dinner one night and ....

"Well, it's about time you two got here! What have you been doing? Dawdling? Leave those shoes outside, Fred. They've got mud on them. And shut the door. Were you born in a barn?

"So, Eleanor, how have you been? I've been meaning to have you over for such a long time. Fred! Take it easy on the chip dip or you'll ruin your dinner. I didn't work over a hot stove all day long to have you nibble like some bird.

"Heard from any of the gang lately? Got a card from the Martins. Yes, they're in Lauderdale again. They go every year to the same spot. What's the matter with you, Fred? You're fidgeting. Of course you have to go. It's down the hall, first door on the left. And I don't want to see a towel in the middle of the floor when you're finished.

"Did you wash your face before you came, Eleanor? I see a dark spot around your mouth. I guess it's a shadow. So, how're your children? If you ask me, I think summer school is great for them. Is everybody hungry? So, why don't we go to the table? You all wash up and I'll take up the food. Don't tell me your hands are clean, Eleanor. I saw you playing with the dog.

"Fred, you sit over there and Eleanor, you can sit with the tall glass of milk. You know you're all elbows when it comes to milk. There now, your host will say grace.

"Fred, I don't see any cauliflower on your plate. Have you ever tried it? Well, try a spoonful. If you don't like it I won't make you finish it, but if you don't try it, you can just forget dessert. And sit up straight or your spine will grow that way.

Oh, what were we talking about? Oh yes, the Gerbers. They sold their house. I mean they took a beating but ... Eleanor, don't talk with food in your mouth. I can't understand a word you're saying. And use your napkin.

At that moment in my fantasy, my son walked into the room.
"How nice of you to come," I said pleasantly.
"Now what did I do," he sighed.

In place of the disrespect Erma Bombeck illustrates in her humorous column, a suggestion with much greater wisdom would be to praise our children five times for every word of criticism. In the words of one wise parent, "A child needs love most when he is most unlovable."

The Baal Shem Tov, founder of the Hasidic movement, was approached by a frustrated parent whose son discarded the pious rituals, and asked for his advice.

"Do you love your son?" asked the Baal Shem Tov.

"Of course," came the reply.

"Then love him more," advised the Baal Shem Tov.

Part of our failure to raise healthy children is that we are often "too busy," in our own lives to give them the time they require. There was a sign in a watchmaker's window: "There's no present like the time."

Dorothy Law Nolte has some wise advice for helping children grow into mature, responsible adults:

Children Learn What They Live

If a child lives with criticism, he learns to condemn.
If a child lives with hostility, he learns to fight.
If a child lives with ridicule, he learns to be shy.
If a child lives with shame, he learns to feel guilty.
If a child lives with tolerance, he learns to be patient.
If a child lives with encouragement, he learns confidence.
If a child lives with praise, he learns to appreciate it.
If a child lives with fairness, he learns justice.
If a child lives with security, he learns to have faith.
If a child lives with approval, he learns to like himself.
If a child lives with acceptance and friendship, he learns
  to find love in the world.[2]

(2) From *Glad to Be Me*, ed. Dov Peretz Elkins, p. 120.

The next "rule" for raising a mature, healthy child is to provide limits. Studies by noted psychologists show that when children grow up with limits, and do not have free reign in all matters of their behavior, they will have higher self-esteem. An effective parent will provide choices, rather than total freedom.

Parents can start in the early years by helping children to select which clothing to wear. Later, they can begin to select their clothing by themselves.

"Rule" number three is to be a good listener – a skill which is useful in all relationships.

The central liturgical statement in Jewish tradition begins with the word "Hear" (*Shema*, in Hebrew).

There is a story of a veteran bartender who was training a young man to be his replacement. The older gentleman told the younger man that he was talking too much, and he was not learning the best techniques of tending bar. When the young man asked for an explanation, the veteran bartender gave this explanation. People don't come to a bar to hear you talk. They come to talk about their personal problems. Your job is to listen. Being a good listener is essential in this profession, and in every profession.

The reason we have two ears and one mouth, it is said, is because we are supposed to listen twice as much as we talk.

The following report is what a nine-year-old child described about the definition of a grandmother.[3]

A Nine-Year-Old Tells Us "What A Grandmother Is"

"A grandmother is a lady who has no children of her own, and so she likes other people's little girls and boys.

"A grandfather is a man-grandmother. He goes for walks with the boys and they talk about fishing and tractors and things like that.

"Grandmas don't have to do anything except: be there. They're old, so they shouldn't play hard or run. It is enough if they drive us to the market where the pretend horse is, and

---

(3) Anonymous.

have lots of dimes handy. Or if they take us for walks, they should slow down past things like pretty leaves or caterpillars. They should never say 'Hurry Up.'

"Usually they are fat, but not too fat to tie kids' shoes. They wear glasses and funny underwear. They can take their teeth and gums out.

"It is better if they don't type or play cards, except with us. They don't have to be smart, only answer questions like, why do dogs hate cats and how come God isn't married. They don't talk baby talk like visitors do, because it is hard to understand. When they read to us they don't skip, or mind if it is the same story again.

"Everybody should try to have one, especially if you don't have television, because grandmas are the only grownups who have time."

The next "rule" is one that grows out of my own upbringing. My parents were loving to my older brother, Armin, and me, and one of the most important ways they showed their love was what I choose to call "Letting-Be."

By that I mean that my parents had enough confidence and love for their two sons that they let us develop in our own paths. They let us make our mistakes, and always trusted that we would come out of whatever difficulties we encountered standing on our feet.

In short, their direction of our lives was more by an unexpressed trust, knowing that we were mature enough to grow in our own way. They "let-be". They let us walk life's path with minimal instruction.

I was always fond of the wisdom of the expert cultural anthropologist, Margaret Mead (1901-1978), who sagaciously taught that the present generation are the natives of our world, and their elders are "foreigners." What she meant by that, I believe, is that the youth of each generation are in so many ways the leaders of our society, and their parents should be smart enough to follow them. That is, let them be.

The job of parents, in bringing up children in an uncertain world is to make themselves dispensable. As Bob Dylan sang, in his classic tune *The Times They are A-changing*, "Your sons and your daughters are beyond your command...."

Another important "rule" is to be the person you hope your children will become. Some call this "modeling." In the words of American philosopher, Ralph Waldo Emerson (1803-1882), "Your actions speak so loud, I can't hear what you're saying." Our children will learn more by watching us than they will by listening to us.

When parents came to me when I served in congregations as rabbi, and complained that their children did not take enough interest in Jewish life as they did, I immediately asked them a series of questions, such as "Did you observe the Sabbath in your home, did you keep the dietary laws, did you attend synagogue worship with regularity, did you fill your home with Jewish art and Jewish books," etc. etc. The message came across very clearly. Their children were so busy watching their parents' behavior that they did not hear what they were saying.

A favorite poem of mine is:[4]

Who Will Be the Zaide of Our Children?

My Zaide lived with us in my parent's home,
He used to laugh, he put me on his knee.
He spoke about his life in Poland,
He spoke with a bitter memory.
He spoke about the soldiers who would beat him.
They laughed at him, they tore his long black coat.

He spoke about a synagogue that they burned down
And the crying that was heard beneath the smoke
But Zaide made us laugh, Zaide made us sing
And Zaide made a kiddush Friday night.

Zaide, oh my Zaide how I love him so
Zaide used to teach me wrong from right
His eyes lit up when he would teach me Torah
He taught me every line so carefully
He spoke about our slavery in Egypt
And how God took us out to make us free.

---

(4)   Anonymous.

But winter went by and summer came along,
I went to camp to run and play
And when I came back home, they said
Zaide's gone, and all his books were packed and stored away
I don't know how or why it came to be.

It happened slowly over many years.
We just stopped being Jewish like my Zaide was
And no one cared enough to shed a tear.

But Zaide made us laugh,
Zaide made us sing
And Zaide made a kiddush Friday night
Zaide, oh my Zaide how I love him so
Zaide used to teach me wrong from right.

Many winters went by, many summers came along
And now my children sit in front of me;
And who will be the "Zaide" of my children
Who will be the "Zaide" if not me
Who will be the "Zaides" of our children
Who will be the "Zaides" if not we . . .

I would like to close this essay with two more of my favorite poems, each of which summarizes all of the "rules" discussed above.

The first is part of a classic poem on "Child-Rearing" by Lebanese-American poet, Kahlil Gibran (1883-1931). The poem is part of Gibran's classic *The Prophet*.

Your children are not your children.
They are the sons and daughters of Life's longing for itself.
They come through you, but not from you,
And though they are with you, yet they belong not to you.

You may give them your love, but not your thoughts,
For they have their own thoughts.
You may house their bodies, but not their souls,
For their souls dwell in the house of tomorrow,
    which you cannot visit, not even in your dreams.

You may strive to be like them,
　　but seek not to make them like you.
For life goes not backward nor tarries with yesterday.

You are the bows from which your children
　　as living arrows are sent forth.

The archer sees the mark upon the path of the infinite,
　　and He bends you with
His might that His arrows may go swift and far.

Let your bending in the archer's hand be for gladness;
For even as He loves the arrow that flies,
　　so He loves also the bow that is stable.

Another favorite poem of mine on the subject of raising (Jewish) children is this one:[5]

All I Got Was Words

When I was young and fancy free,
My folks had no fine clothes for me
All I got was words –
　　Gott tzu danken
　　Gott vet geben
　　Zoln rnir leben un zein gezunt

When I was wont to travel far,
They didn't provide for me a car
All I got was words –
　　Geh gezunt
　　Geh pamelech
　　Hub a glickliche rayze

I wanted to increase my knowledge
But they couldn't send me to college
All I got was words –

_____

(5)　Anonymous.

Hub saychel
Zei nischt kein narr
Torah iz di beste schorah

The years have flown –
The world has turned,
Things I've gotten, things I've learned,
Yet I remember –

Zog dem emes
Gib tzedakah
Hub rachmonas
Zei a mensch!

All I got was words.

| 5 |

When Bad Things Happen to Good People – Dealing with Evil

The problem of evil is as old as the Bible. The Book of Job struggles with the issues of Job, a prosperous man of excellent piety, who lost his wife and family, suffers from several diseases, and loses his possessions. Yet Job still refuses to curse God. Despite lengthy poetic dialogue among Job's friend, Job and even God, God's ways with humans remain mysterious and inscrutable.

One of the best-known theologians of the twentieth century was the late Rabbi Milton Steinberg. Steinberg listed a series of theories for the presence of evil in moral terms.

First is the most obvious, which is that evil is the result of sin. One is punished for wrongdoing, even when the person seems to be not culpable. Perhaps the sin may have escaped notice, or the punishment is not associated as a consequence of an offense.

In the Jewish liturgy we say "because of our sins we were exiled from our land."

Another theory is that evil or bad things come not from any individual iniquity, but from that of the community.

In the Talmud we read, "Sufferings come upon the world only when there are wicked people in the world...but once the power of destruction is unleashed, it does not differentiate between the righteous and the wicked."[1] In other words, the mouth may swallow the poison, but the whole body suffers.

A third theory undergirded by morality is that humans are moral creatures by nature, and they have free choice. Therefore, when a person commits a crime, that person chooses to bring evil on the world. God is not the culprit, but the perpetrator is.

When Rabbi Abraham Joshua Heschel was asked to explain the evil of the Holocaust with this question: How could a loving God have permitted such evil, his answer was: You are asking

(1) Bava Kama 60A.

the wrong question. The correct question is: How could humans have done such things? In other words, evil is human-made, not divinely created.

When Adam and Eve ate the apple from the tree of knowledge of good and evil, they knew what they were doing. We humans have free will, we can choose to do good or evil. Christianity calls it the Fall of Man. Some call it, rather, a "Fall Upward," since once they came out of Paradise, they were free to do whatever they wanted to do, good or bad.

The final theory based on a moral theory is that we would not know what evil is if we did not know what good is. Good is only good in relation to bad.

Another line of thought goes like this:

Evil, trouble, punishment, brings out the good in human beings.

The character of human beings is such that it needs prodding, motivation to improve things. When there is danger, it brings out courage. Love is strongest and deepest when in trial and difficulty.

When there is disease, or natural disasters such as an earthquake or a hurricane, it encourages humans to struggle to improve the situation. We become God's partner in perfecting the world.

When a woman suffers pain in childbirth, it is in the service of a good result.

When an artist or an author struggles to create, something good can result. Milton's blindness was a factor in his creativity, and the cause of his beautiful poem, "On His Blindness." The enslavement of our people in ancient Egypt ultimately ennobled the character of our people.

The famous psychologist, Carl Jung, wrote: "All creativeness in the realm of the spirit as well as every psychic advance of man arises from a state of mental suffering."

In Jewish theology we have a concept of *"hevlay haMashiah,"* – the pangs that precede the coming of the Messianic Age.

The Midrash teaches[2] "As the olive does not lend precious oil except under pressure, so Israel does not bring forth its highest virtues except through adversity."

(2) Exodus Rabbah 1:1, on Exodus 27:20.

The next idea is that tough times can help to test the stuff of which people are made. Some people do not know how strong they are until they have an adversary against whom they contend.

There are spiritual laws of nature which cannot be disobeyed or violated. There are no exceptions. Not even God can change such laws. The Midrash teaches,[3] "If it were possible, I would even now dismiss the Angel of Death, but death against humanity has already been decreed by Me, hence it must remain."

In other words, if we sin, we suffer. It is in the nature of the universe since sinful actions are automatically punished. When someone touches a high-tension wire, he is immediately punished. Not because an engineer at the transformer is angry at him, but it is by the very nature of electricity.

"Of itself the punishment comes upon the evildoers and the blessings upon the doers of good."[4]

A person who defies the law of gravity by jumping off the roof of a tall building is punished, not because God is angry at the person, but because s/he ignored the law of nature. It is the same with spiritual laws. One who frequently slanders others finds that s/he loses many friends.

Next, there are theories of the presence of evil, in metaphysical terms. Evil is not real, it is merely the absence of God. Cold, for example, is the absence of heat.

Maimonides[5] taught that darkness is only the absence of light, it is not an entity in itself. Evil is an illusion. The Christian Scientist will argue that there is no pain. Those who think they are in pain are mistaken.

These are perhaps the easiest theories to dismiss. People do die from exposure from cold, it is not an illusion. People do stumble and fall in the dark. Cars skid on wet roads and accidents occur, i.e. wet is not the absence of dry.

There is a theory which accounts for evil that it is only something temporary, and in the end it is destined to be transcended and retrieved. Not very convincing.

(3) Louis Ginzberg, Legends of the Jews, III, p. 107.
(4) Deuteronomy Rabbah 4.
(5) 1138-1204, Spain and Egypt.

Next, there are those who argue that evil will be compensated and made good in life after death.

The philosopher Hasdai Crescas[6] wrote: "There is only one answer and that is *olam haba* (the future world), because you will never sustain a human being by telling him to think that evil is not evil, that it is the absence of good, and that God is not responsible for it."

Still another argument is that pain is useful because it tells us that something is wrong. There is physical pain (illness) and moral pain (pangs of conscience) as a sign that a person requires therapy. Pain is one of the costs of being alive.

Finally, the only answer to the question of evil, which has stumped teachers and philosophers for centuries, is that the question of "Why is there evil in the world?" is unanswerable, inscrutable. It is an enigma for us. God alone may know the answer, but we mortals have no reasonable explanation.

Our ancestors understood this unsolvable dilemma: "It is not in our power to explain either the tranquility of the wicked or the sufferings of the upright."[7]

As noted, from ancient days to the present, human mortals do not have an adequate answer to the question of why there is evil in the world. "Though he slay me, yet will I trust in him."[8]

Several modern scholars have expressed a similar frustration.

"That God should put upon men the responsibility for conformity with moral law, and yet leave them with an inclination toward forms of behavior that are definitely evil, is an unresolved paradox. '*Oi li miyozri, oi li miyizri* – Woe is me by reason of my Creator and woe is me by reason of my evil inclination!'[9] Thus our sages gave expression to the tragic dilemma that in every generation raises doubts in men's minds as to the reality of a good God."[10]

Solomon Schechter, in his *Aspects of Rabbinic Theology*, writes: "There is really no general view on suffering. All of

---

(6)   1340-1410, Spain.
(7)   Pirke Avot 4:19.
(8)   Job 13:15.
(9)   Talmud Berakhot 61A.
(10)   Mordechai M. Kaplan, *The Future of the American Jew*, pp. 238-9.

the views offered are simply meant to pacify the mind of the afflicted person so that he should not become despondent and that it may help him to bear his lot courageously."

There is a Hasidic story about a rabbi who was asked by his pupils to remove the existence of evil. The rabbi suggested that the students take a broom and sweep the darkness from a cellar. They tried, but to no avail. Then the rabbi told them to take sticks and beat vigorously at the darkness to drive it out. That too failed. Then he told them to go into the cellar and protest against the cellar and shout curses. That also failed. Finally he said, let each of you meet the challenge of darkness by lighting a candle. Each disciple went down into the cellar, lit a candle, and the darkness was driven out. The role of the Jew, explained the rabbi, is to be a light unto the Nations, to remove the darkness of prejudice, ignorance, hatred, disease and war.

Rabbi Menahem ben Shlomo HaMeiri[11] in his commentary on Pirke Avot wrote that "The Lord created the evil impulse, but He created Torah and repentance as its remedy."

There is a Hasidic teaching that people are God's language. We are here to do God's work: to feed the hungry, clothe the naked, heal the sick.

In 1981, Rabbi Harold Kushner published a book out of the agony of losing a son. The book, *When Bad Things Happen to Good People*, helps millions of people find, if not an answer, at least a modicum of comfort.

Not everyone was able to accept Kushner's thesis, that there is randomness in the world that is unpredictable and mostly not preventable – such as earthquakes, tornadoes, disease, traffic accidents. In some future day, science may help us to reduce the randomness of the world, but there will always be some terrible things that may come our way.

The role of God, says Kushner, is not to prevent pain and suffering, but to help us get through such times. God is not with evil-doers, God is with the victims. God does not control human choices, so anyone can, at will, take a gun and end someone's life. That is the decision of humans, who have free will.

Judaism's role, taught Rabbi Kushner, is not to explain evil,

(11)   1249-1315, Spain.

but to help people learn how to live with it. Jews write theology to explain things to us and others.

"My theology," taught Kushner, "is not concerned with defending God or with attacking God. My theology is concerned with helping people. When people hurt, I want to use religion and belief and faith to bring them comfort."

Another scholar put it this way: "God is not in the accident, God is in the ambulance."

| 6 |

Human Sexuality: One Jew's Personal View

I want to share some personal thoughts as well as some historical and sociological views meshed together in an integrated way on the subject of human sexuality, from the point of view of a Jew, of a person who has struggled with the problem as a Jewish theologian and Rabbi, who was married for eighteen years, who was divorced and remarried, struggling with interpersonal relationships in a new and completely different way.

We know that the traditions of sexuality that have come out of Judaism in the past, as well as those that have come out of all of traditional morality, no longer can stand us in the same strong sense of wellbeing and security that they had for so many centuries. We are living in a world in which Matthew Arnold said, "The old is destroyed; the old world is gone and yet the new world has not yet been born."

We know what we don't want anymore, but none of us is certain what we really do want out of interpersonal relationships, out of marriage, out of sexuality. Just as Adam said to Eve as they were banished from the Garden of Eden – he turned to her and he said, "You know, Eve, we're living in an age of transition." And I suppose that ever since that time we've been living in ages of transition, when old worlds were crumbling and new worlds were trying to be born. Yet even as they are born they somehow crumble and become replaced by something newer, presumably better, but not always.

I sought to etch out a set of guidelines for a modern person, from a Jewish point of view, but hopefully having universal applicability. There are a number of principles, because no one person can tell another what to do; neither as a Rabbi or as a counselor or as a friend have I ever told anyone what they must or should do, or perform ... or a way that they must behave, but some general guidelines to help us understand and provide some directions. For even though the old world and the old standards may be gone, and the new ones are not always acceptable to us, nevertheless, some form of guidelines, even if temporary, are absolutely necessary for a human being to exist. We cannot function in a vacuum. And then I found, after perusing the literature on sexuality, and some of the modern Jewish theologians, that what I had done, simply, was to reinvent the wheel; that some of my colleagues and teachers had indeed drawn up several codes of ethics for human sexuality in our day. So what I present to you is an amalgam of some of my own thoughts, some of the words of the sages who were grappling with this problem in our day.

And so I present to you a number of principles with some comments and hopefully some elucidation that will help us understand them more deeply.

Principle number one: Personal happiness is a legitimate goal for human beings in general. Sexual experience is a major source of pleasure and wellbeing for men and women and its successful functioning is a proper objective in marriage. Coming from a tradition as I do, sexuality was looked upon as the way Judaism looks so positively upon the physical experience between a male and a female. Medieval mystics compared the experience of ecstasy in the act of intercourse with the deepest kind of ecstasy that one reaches in a state of nirvana, almost, of union with God. So man's union with God is the comparison that some of the Jewish medieval sages compare to man's union with woman and woman's union with man in the sexual act.

In a tradition which says that the world was created as a good place, and the physical contact between human beings is a positive and wonderful and pleasurable experience, I can only reemphasize that important aspect of our understanding of sexuality as it is enunciated in my tradition. The medieval mystic Nahmanides wrote: "We who are the descendants of those who received the Torah believe that God created everything – everything – as His wisdom dictated, and He created nothing containing obscenity or ugliness, for if we say that sexual relations are obscene, it would follow that the sexual organs are obscene, and how could God create something containing a blemish or a defect?" That is the fundamental principle out of which sexual understanding emerges in the tradition of a people that has suffered persecution, and nevertheless has held onto a sense of optimism about life, about the beauty of the physical world, and that reminds us in an ancient passage in the Talmud, written some two thousand years ago, that he who denies himself the physical pleasures of the world will be called to account at the end of his life for not having taken advantage of those wonderful opportunities that he or she missed during the lifetime.

Principle number two: Marriage is intended not merely for the procreation of the race, but also for companionship and love. Many places in Jewish legal literature we find the encouragement to marry even when there is no possibility of bearing children.

Principle number three: The equality of men and women, which has been a basic thrust of the Jewish tradition, though not always carried out in all of its details – this general stress of equality between men and women has not yet been fully achieved in any society – it must be carried forward until its legitimate goals are achieved. The Jewish tradition is almost synonymous with freedom, and for any people, any oppressed group, whether it be religious, racial, sexual, or other, is an anathema to accept oppression for a people that has struggled for four thousand years to bring freedom and peace and a vision of the ancient prophets to the entire human world.

Principle number four: Mutuality in love and respect are the foundations of marriage. Domination of each partner by the other erases the equality which is at the heart of the marriage relationship. But the partners are not discrete individuals, each concerned basically with maintaining his or her own independence, and therefore jealously minimizing the points of contact with the other. On the contrary, the relationship of the two partners in a marriage is conceived of as two circles intersecting with each other, constantly striving to come closer so that they may possess a larger area in common.

Fritz Perls, who comes out of the Jewish tradition, the founder of Gestalt therapy, who was attached in philosophy more to Zen Buddhism than he was to his own heritage and called himself, therefore, a Zen Judist, created the so called

Gestalt prayer, which the new morality hails as its credo:

"I do my thing, and you do your thing. I am not in this world to live up to your expectations, and you are not in this world to live up to mine. I am I and you are you."

Wonderful so far, the independence there. Who can deny motherhood and apple pie?

"And if by chance we find each other, it's beautiful. If not, it cannot be helped."

There's a great deal of wisdom embedded in the words of Perls, but there is more missing than there is present, and so some clever poet created his own form of the Gestalt prayer:

"If I just do my thing and you just do yours, we stand in danger of losing each other, and ourselves. I am not in this world to live up to your expectations, but I am in this world to confirm you, as a unique human being, and to be confirmed by you. We are fully ourselves only in relation to each other. The I detached from a Thou disintegrates. I do not find you by chance; I find you by an act of life, of reaching out. Rather than passively letting things happen to me, I can act intentionally to make them happen. I must begin with myself, true, but I must not end with myself. The truth begins with two."

A more realistic and more Jewish point of view, I think, than Zen Judistic.

Principle number five: Sex is not a sin; marriage is not a prison; divorce is not a crime. I look upon my divorce as unfortunate. The Talmud tells us that when a bride and groom of youth end their marital relationship, the very altar in the sanctuary sheds tears. But I also look upon it as an opportunity to grow and learn, and become a better and fuller person, and to establish the kind of relationship that I think I deserve. My ex-spouse feels the very same way, and so with Margaret Mead, we might say that in life there often have to be serial relationships, and marriage may not be meant for a lifetime. The last years of my serving in congregations, young people would come to me for the premarital interview and would ask to change the last few words, instead of saying, "Until death do us part," to substitute the expression, "Until I find someone I like better."

I am sure that that extreme is not how far I would go, but I do think that the wholesome notion that divorce is a valid option as a last resort, is certainly a Biblically acceptable, respectable position.

I think what we are missing in today's society is the preparation one needs for marriage. I knew nothing about interpersonal relationships or marriage when I was twenty-two years old, standing under the bridal canopy. I think we need – and here the churches and the synagogues are more at fault than anyone – much more family life education, preparatory education, so that people understand what it means, at that stage in their life, to enter into a lifelong commitment.

In the Jewish tradition there's a wonderful genre of literature comparable to the so-called ethnic jokes that are found among other peoples, only we do it with a little more respectable and wholesome viewpoint (excuse my chauvinism). It's called the stories of the wise – euphemistically so called, wise men of Chelm – really the fools of Chelm. One of the stories tells about the people who lived in a village at the top of a hill and people kept falling down the hill and getting hurt.

The council of sages of Chelm got together and decided how to solve this serious medical problem. People were always falling down and getting hurt, and the great decision that resulted is what we do when we create mental health clinics, and we deal with people who have already suffered the problems of failure – in sexuality, in marriage, in life, generally. And what we need is not a hospital at the bottom of the hill, but a school at the top of the hill.

One minister was asked what he thinks of Christianity over the past two thousand years and his response was, "I really don't know. We haven't tried it yet." We all have great ideals that we don't live up to, but nevertheless we need those ideals as a guiding spirit to reach towards.

The next principle is that each human being is an arena in which body, mind, and spirit are interwoven and inseparable. Hence, love and sex are indivisible in a complete, satisfying man-woman relationship, for only then is the total human personality involved. To sanctify love and denigrate sex, or conversely, to cultivate sex and scorn love, is to invite schizophrenia.

The next guideline is that we must recapture the conviction that marriage is a union involving not two but three partners – a man, a woman and God. Our generation needs to learn anew that the old truth that marriage is a compact in which husband and wife are bound together by a sacred duty that goes far beyond the drive of physical infatuation or the economic and social advantages of living together. We must reject the dangerous and often insincere doctrine that love, the physical attraction of two persons, is an all-sufficient condition for marriage, and that the absence of compatibility in religious backgrounds, in education, in interests, in ideals or temperament is an irrelevant consideration. I will not go into greater detail into any of these particular requirements, but I think that certainly the Hollywood notion of romance is not a sufficient ideal for a union of two people in marriage.

The next guideline is that because the love-sex relationship has long range consequences both for the individuals and for generations yet unborn, the best state in which it can take place is the stability and permanence that only the marriage institution can offer. This has always been recognized, and in spite of all the onslaughts against it, the marriage institution remains unique and irreplaceable, especially with regard to the raising of children. We know of no other way that comes close to the success of providing for a newborn infant. A mother and a father who are models of a loving relationship create a happy, healthy, emotionally mature individual.

And lastly, as Rabbi Robert Gordis wrote, "the family is the bridge linking the individual and society, each influencing and benefitting the other. The home in which sexual activity attains its highest potential as love is the greatest single instrument for teaching the truth that human happiness must be sought and can be found only in adhering to both elements in the great ancient injunction of Rabbi Hillel in the Talmud who said, 'If I am not for myself, who will be for me? But if I am for myself alone, of what good am I?'"[1]

---

(1)   *Love and Sex: A Modern Jewish Perspective*, 1978, pp. 150-1.

| 7 |

Polarity and Paradox

L ife seems filled with polarities and paradoxes.
In the liturgy of the Jewish High Holidays, there seems to be a clear case of both.

The polarities are obvious: life and death, good and evil, kindness and cruelty.

Before we plunge into the polarities and paradoxes of the Jewish High Holidays, let us examine what the famous psychologist, Abraham Maslow (1908-1970) who is well-known for his research on healthy people[1], wrote about our topic.

Abraham Maslow.

"The dichotomy between selfishness and unselfishness disappears altogether in healthy people because in principle every act is *both selfish and unselfish*. Our subjects are simultaneously very spiritual and very pagan and sensual even to the point where sexuality becomes a path to the spiritual and religious. Duty cannot be contrasted with pleasure, nor work with play, when work is play, and the person doing his duty and being virtuous is simultaneously seeking his pleasure and being happy. If the most socially identified people are themselves also the most individualistic people, of what use is it to retain the polarity? If the most mature are also childlike? And if the most ethical and moral people are also the lustiest and most animalistic?"[2]

With Maslow's understanding of polarities, let us examine some of the concepts of the liturgy of the Jewish High Holidays.

The Midrash tells the following legend:

When we sound the shofar, God moves from the throne

---

(1) Whereas most psychologists study people who are unwell.
(2) Quoted in *Glad To Be Me*, ed. Elkins, p. 83.

Ideas

of justice to the throne of mercy.[3]

In other words, God has two thrones, or two qualities, justice and mercy. On the face of it, these two qualities are polar opposites. Yet God exhibits both. As Maslow's "healthy person," one individual can possess two polar opposites. If God can, so can we.

Every human judge must utilize both of these qualities at different times. Sometimes a judge must employ the quality of justice, and at other times the quality of mercy. The decision will depend on the situation.

If a judge frees evil people, using compassion alone, society suffers. If a judge sends every first-offender to jail, the judge turns the world into a huge prison. Making each decision is a balancing act between justice and mercy.

Yet how can one person exhibit both polarities, opposite qualities – tough and soft, hard and lenient, enforce the law and bend the law?

The American poet Carl Sandburg (1878-1967) described Abraham Lincoln in these words to a Joint Session of Congress on the 150th anniversary of Lincoln's birth:

> "Not often in the story of mankind does a man arrive on earth who is both steel and velvet, who is as hard as rock and soft as drifting fog, who holds in his heart and mind the paradox of terrible storm and peace unspeakable and perfect. Here and there across centuries come reports of men alleged to have these contrasts. And the incomparable Abraham Lincoln...is an approach if not a perfect realization of this character."

Similar to the riddle in the Book of Judges, when Samson had killed a lion with his bare hands.[4] Later he saw that a swarm of bees settled in its body and deposited honey there. He challenged his friends with a riddle, which took them an entire week to unlock: "Out of the strong came something sweet."

The riddle was difficult to decipher because it is rare when both something strong and sweet cohabit the same place. Steel wrapped in velvet. A lion and honey. An Israeli sabra plant

(3)   Vayikra Rabbah 29: 3, 4, 6, and 10.
(4)   Judges 14:5-6.

(prickly outside and soft inside).

Thus the midrash in the legend of the shofar. God can do it, and there is a hint that humans can make it happen when the shofar is blown – God arises from the throne of judgment and sits on the throne of mercy.

Many years ago a management consultant and university professor, Douglas McGregor (1906-1964) wrote a book titled *The Human Side of Enterprise*. The author put forth the idea that the best style of management is a combination of a caring side and a tough side. Similar to good parenting, there are times to be demanding and a time to be caring and loving.

Another example in Jewish liturgy of a necessary and useful polarity is contained in one of the most popular prayers – the *Alenu*, which concludes most worship.

There are two poles in this prayer – loyalty to our people, and loyalty to the world. In other words, there is the particular and the universal.

The first paragraph points to our particular people, when we thank God for not making us as all the other nations. The second paragraph makes no mention of Jews or Judaism, when we ask God to repair the entire world "under the sovereignty of the Almighty, when all humanity will call upon Your name. Then the Lord shall be Sovereign over all the earth."

The tension between these two poles appears in Jewish life in many ways. Jews are often asked whether their first loyalty is to the country in which they live, or to the religion/peoplehood to which they swear allegiance. Some opponents of Jews even accuse Jews of "dual loyalty," and question the loyalty of Jews to their country (outside of Israel, of course). Justice Louis Brandeis formulated a statement which offered an answer to this charge, when he said that the more loyal we are to Judaism and to the Jewish People, the better Americans we are. In saying this, Brandeis integrated both polarities – the religious/ethnic side and the national side of our people.

Jews face this same dilemma when they are faced with these polar questions:

Shall we send our children to a public school or to a Jewish day school?

Should we donate our charity dollars more to secular causes

(museums, hospitals, universities) or to specifically Jewish causes that assist Jews and Jewish organizations in need?

The tension between these two poles has been compared to the tension of a tightrope wire that an acrobat walks – neither too tight nor too loose.

Another interesting example in Jewish liturgy is the tension between the following two poles: *"Keva"* and *"Kavannah"* (the fixed liturgy as opposed to augmented liturgy with additional creative poems and other modern prayers).

In the Talmud,[5] Rabbi Shimon says "Do not make your prayer *"keva,"* a fixed routine. In the biblical Book of Psalms (96:1) we read, "Sing unto the Lord a new song."

Rabbi Abraham Joshua Heschel writes about this problem, of the tension between fixed prayers and devotion (*keva* and *kavannah*) in *Moral Grandeur and Spiritual Audacity*:

"There is a specific difficulty with Jewish prayer. There are laws: fixed texts. On the other hand, prayer is worship of the heart, the outpouring of the soul, a matter of devotion. Thus, Jewish prayer is guided by two opposite principles: order and outburst, regularity and spontaneity, uniformity and individuality, law and freedom. These principles are the two poles about which Jewish prayer revolves. Since each of the two moves in the opposite direction, equilibrium can be maintained only if both are of equal force. However, the pole of regularity usually proves to be stronger than the pole of spontaneity, and as a result, there is a perpetual danger of prayer becoming a mere habit, a mechanical performance, an exercise in repetitiousness. The fixed pattern and regularity of our services tends to stifle the spontaneity of devotion. Our great problem, therefore, is now not to let the principle of regularity impair the power of devotion. It is a problem that concerns not only prayer but the whole sphere of Jewish observance. He who is not aware of this central difficulty is a simpleton; he who offers a simple solution is a quack."

Some of the prayers that were originally added to the fixed

(5) Pirke Avot 2:18.

structure of the liturgy, such as *Adon Olam, Yigdal, U'Netaneh Tokef,* and many others, were once optional. Today no one would dare omit them.

Let's examine another polarity. That is the poles of selfishness and selflessness.

A healthy person takes care of her/his own needs, and then can take care of others (See the essay on self-esteem).

Everyone has an innate need to help and love. If that is true, when you give to others, you are also giving to yourself – fulfilling your need to give and serve.

Maslow gave the example of giving up his dessert to his child because he has the pleasure of watching her eat it, and that pleasure is greater than eating it himself. Is that selfless or selfish? The distinctions blur.

People who take good care of themselves and meet their own needs are the best ones to trust to serve others. A person who is so needy and hungry cannot really have enough self-esteem to share oneself. One who serves on every board and committee and neglects one's own family and one's health, even one's business, is doing a disservice to those s/he pretends to serve, and no one gains.

Many examples of similar polarities in Jewish literature abound. Here are some examples:

You are not obliged to complete the work, but neither are you free to neglect it. (This is an example of the polarity of apathy and responsibility).

There is the truism that the long way is actually the short way.

Then there is in Hasidic literature a description of a person who should keep two quotations in his pockets. In one pocket should be the quotation "For my sake the world was created."[6] In the other pocket should be the quotation "I am but dust and ashes."[7] This is the polarity between healthy self-pride and humility.

In a passage in Pirke Avot (3:19) we read that "Everything is

(6)   Sanhedrin 4:5.
(7)   Genesis 18:27.

foreseen, yet freedom of choice is given."

In another Talmudic passage we find the sage Hillel saying "ascending is really descending, and descending is actually ascending."[8]

In a Midrashic passage we find that the angels debated whether to have humans created from Heaven or Earth. Their decision was to take a little of each. Thus, humans are both material and spiritual. "God formed Adam of the dust of the ground"[9] – as one of the creatures of the lower realm. "And He blew into his nostrils the breath of life"[10] – as one of the creatures of the upper realm.[11]

One of the famous sage Hillel's best known sayings is:[12]

"If I am not for myself, who will be? But if I am for myself alone, what am I?"

Here again is the polarity of self-care and care for others.

A Solution

How do we explain the illogic of the fact that both something and its opposite are both true, both necessary, complementary and both are required for healthy living?

One answer is found in the Torah:[13] "The hidden things are known only to God, and the observable things are for us and our posterity."

A medieval Jewish philosopher once wrote that "If I knew God, I would be God."[14] In other words, some answers are only open to divinity.

One of the most interesting solutions comes from Professor Mircea Eliade (1907-1986) who wrote in his book *The Two and the One,* that life's polarities and paradoxes "have the aim of reminding men that the ultimate reality, the sacred, the divine,

(8)   Midrash Leviticus Rabbah.
(9)   Genesis 2:7.
(10)   Ibid.
(11)   Midrash Leviticus Rabbah 9,9.
(12)   Avot 1:14.
(13)   Deuteronomy 29:28.
(14)   Rabbi Joseph Albo, 1380-1444, Spain, Sefer *Ha-Ikkarim.*

defy all possibilities of rational comprehension;

• That the *Grund* (reality) can only be grasped as a mystery or a paradox, that the divine conception cannot be conceived as a sum of qualities and virtues but as an absolution freedom, beyond Good and Evil;

• That the divine, absolute and transcendent are qualitatively different from the human, relative and immediate.

In a word, these myths, rites and theories involving the *coincidentia oppositorum* teach men that the best way of apprehending God or the ultimate reality is to cease, if only for a few seconds, considering and imagining divinity in terms of immediate experience; such an experience could only perceive fragments and tensions!"

A simpler way of expressing this idea is in the Chinese language and philosophy, in which the two poles of cosmic energy, the yin (or negative) and yang (positive) are represented in ideograms indicating the sunny and shady sides of a hill. The yin and the yang in Chinese tradition are associated with masculine and feminine, firm and yielding, strong and weak, light and dark, rising and falling, heaven and earth. They are recognized in everyday matters as cooking, as the spicy and the bland.

As the English philosopher Alan Watts (1915-1973) has written:[15] "The act of life is not seen as holding to yang and banishing yin, but as keeping the two in balance because there cannot be one without the other."

The American psychologist E. Paul Torrance (1915-2003), best known for his research in creativity, taught that the most creative people are both masculine and feminine (in style), independent in their thinking and at the same time most open to suggestions; more playful and more serious, more humorous and more grave.[16]

The American novelist F. Scott Fitzgerald (1896-1940) expressed our idea extremely clearly when he said that "The test of a first-rate intelligence is the ability to hold two opposed ideas in mind at the same time and still retain the ability to function."

The Talmud holds the same view. Almost every page contains

(15)   *Tao: The Watercourse Way*, pp. 19-21.
(16)   *The Search for Satori and Creativity*, p. 55.

contradictory views, and frequently there is no resolution. The attitude of the Talmudic rabbis seems to be that even though there may be contradictory views on a subject – one says white and his colleague says black – both views are recorded. Often one opinion is selected as the one to follow. This does not mean that the opposite is not also valid. However, in action, one way is chosen.

There is a statement in the Talmud, which appears often, that states that "*Ayleh v'ayleh divray Elohim hayyim*," that is, "both this opinion and its opposite are the words of the living God." How remarkable! The rabbis are suggesting that two opposing opinions are both divinely ordained. The rabbis are careful to record both opposing opinions, so that future generations have the option of selecting a different point of view. And there is a clear recognition that both opposing views have validity. "Both this opinion and its opposite are the words of the living God."

If all disputants in a debate would acknowledge the truth of the other side, what a better world we would be living in.

| 8 |

Creativity in the Jewish Tradition

Introduction

Charles Lamb once was asked where he got the material for one of his essays. He answered that he had milked 300 cows for it, but the butter was his own. In other words, there are many sources, but the synthesis is mine. The difference between a scholar and a plagiarist: A scholar copies 100 sources, plagiarist one source. That is, creativity is often a new synthesis of old material.

With creativity, like humor, you see something in a new way.

Scholarly Sources on Creativity

Carl Rogers

"The mainspring of creativity appears to be the same tendency which we discover so deeply as the curative force in psychotherapy – man's tendency to actualize himself, to become his potentialities. By this I mean the directional trend which is evident in all organic and human life – the urge to expand, extend, develop, mature – the tendency to express and activate all the capacities of the organism, or the self."[1]

Abraham Maslow

Maslow created a revolution. In psychology, he studied *healthy* people, whereas most psychologists study neurotic, sick, people.

"Most human beings lose this as they become enculturated, but some few individuals seem either to retain this fresh and naive, direct way of looking at life, or if they have lost it, as most people do, they later recover it.

"This creativeness appears in some of our subjects not in the usual forms of writing books, composing music, or producing

---

(1) Carl Rogers, *On Becoming A Person* (Boston: Houghton, Mifflin, 1961) pp. 350-1 (Chap. 19, "Toward a Theory of Creativity" 347 ff).

artistic objects, but rather may be much more humble. It is as if this special type of creativeness, being an expression of a healthy personality, is projected out upon the world or touches whatever activity the person is engaged in. In this sense there can be creative shoemakers or carpenters or clerks. Whatever one does can be done with a certain attitude, a certain spirit that arises out of the nature of the character of the person performing the act. One can even see creatively as the child does."[2]

Notes On Creativity In The Jewish Tradition

I. Creation Unfinished

"In His goodness God renews the creation every day continually."[3]

Humans are *"shutaf be-maasay beresheit* – partners in creation."[4]

The words, "There is yet much more work to be done", mean that the process of the world's creation is only in its infancy.[5]

The Hasidic master, Rabbi Simhah Bunam[6] said: "The Lord created the world in a state of beginning" (*Beresheit*). The universe is always in an uncompleted state, in the form of its beginning. It is not like a vessel at which the master works and he finishes it; it requires continuous labor and unceasing renewal by creative forces. Were there a second's pause by these forces, the universe would return to primeval chaos."[7]

Said the Besht:[8] It is written:[9] "They are new every morning; great is thy faith."

A person should believe that each day the world is re-created, and that he is reborn each morning. His faith will then be increased, and he will take a fresh interest daily in his

---

(2) Abraham Maslow, *Motivation and Personality*, 1954, p. 223.
(3) Siddur *Le-el barukh...* Hertz Siddur, p. 114.
(4) Talmud, Shabbat 10A.
(5) Midrash, Pesikta Rabbati, 6, 25a; *Talmudic Anthology,* p. 86.
(6) Poland, 1765-1827.
(7) *Hasidic Anthology*, p. 62.
(8) Rabbi Israel the **B**aal **Sh**em **T**ov, Ukraine 1700-1760.
(9) Lamentations 3:23.

service to the Lord.[10]

Today is the birthday of the world. (Rosh Hashana liturgy – *Hayom Harat Olam*). That is, every day the world begins again, anew.

II. Affirmations and Visualization
1) All things in the world follow thought.[11]
2) All that ends in deed is first in thought.[12]
3) The power of thinking has two servants: the power of memory and the power of imagination.[13] (Cognitive, affective; right brain, left brain).
4) Said Reb Nahman of Bratslav – We are made in God's image *(demut)*. *Demut* can mean "imagination." The way we are like God is that we have His imagination; we are similar to God in that we have imagination, like God.

III. Endless Search
1) Concept of midrash – updating, contemporaneity.
2) Darash – search, discover, read between lines, embellish.
3) Turn it over and over, for all is in it.[14]
4) The Torah has 70 faces (aspects, interpretations).[15]

Examples of liturgical innovation
Piyyut – a collection of medieval poems added to the traditional liturgy. Throughout the centuries, rabbis insisted that the liturgy included both standard passages, and new, creative religious poetry (*keva* and *kavannah*, i.e., the fixed liturgy and new insertions to increase relevance and intensive concentration).

One who toils in Torah and discovers in it new meanings that are true, contributes new Torah which is treasured by the

---

(10)   *Hasidic Anthology*, p. 62.
(11)   Midrash, Sitre Torah, i, 155a (*Talmudic Anthology*. p. 260).
(12)   Lekha Dodi, Siddur.
(13)   Zohar, iv, 247b (*Talmudic Anthology*. p. 260).
(14)   Pirke Avot (5:26).
(15)   Talmud.

congregation of Israel.[16]

Concept of Written Torah and Oral Torah

Everything stated by a scholar of every future age was already stated at Sinai to Moses.[17] (Legitimization of expansion of Torah).

Hasidic Midrash:

Beresheit – creation story:

Rabbi Wolf Strikover finds these hints in the first verse of the Torah (Ber. 1:1), using the word *Beresheit* in Hebrew as an acronym:

1) *Bitahon*, or trust,
2) *Ratson*, or will,
3) *Ahavah*, or love,
4) *Shetikah*, or silence,
5) *Yirah*, or fear,
6) *Torah*, or learning.

These are the most important essentials in the character of a person of goodness.

Bara (create) reminds us of the three most important material needs:

1) *Bara*, suggests children, from "bar", son,
2) *Bara*, health, from bari, healthy,
3) *Bara*, food, from bar, grain.

Bara Elohim Et – the last Hebrew letters of these words spell Emet, truth. The creation can rest only upon truth.[18]

Resh Lakish said: The Torah is white fire and black fire (black on white, letters on parchment). White fire is holier than black fire. (The spaces are more important than the letters.) Namely, imagination, what we fill in, is most important.[19]

---

(16)   Zohar, i. 243a (*Talmudic Anthology,* p. 504).
(17)   Midrash, Shemot Rabbah 28:6.
(18)   *Hasidic Anthology*, p. 62
(19)   Ancient Hebrew readers had to fill in vowels, and brought more to the book than was there. (Talmud).

IV. Personal growth, renewal

Rabbi Tzvi Hirsh Zidichov (1763-1831, Ukraine) once said to his Hasidim: "When one rises in the morning and sees that God has returned his soul to him and that he has become a new creature, he should sing to God. My holy master Rabbi Menahem Mendel had a Hasid who, whenever he came to the words in the morning prayer: 'My God, the soul you have placed in me is pure', danced and broke into a song of praise."[20]

"When we do not believe that God renews each day the work of creation, then our prayer and fulfillment of the commands (*mitzvot*) becomes old, routine and boring. As it says in the Psalm,[21] 'Do not cast me off when I am old'; that is, do not let my world become old."[22]

"In order to perfect oneself, one must renew oneself day by day."[23]

V. Physical Propagation

Rabbi Eliezer taught: "A person who does not engage in the propagation of the species is like someone who has shed blood."[24]

VI. Flexibility, Adaptability

At all times let a person be supple as the reed and not rigid as the cedar: A reed, when all the winds come and blow upon it, bends with them; when the winds are still, the reed is again upright in its place. And the end of this reed? Its good fortune is to be used as the pen that writes the Torah scroll.

The cedar, however, does not remain standing in its place; for as soon as the south wind blows, it uproots it and tears it down. And the end of the cedar? Loggers cane upon it and chop it up and use it to cover the housetops – and what remains, they cast to the flames. [25]

---

(20)   Buber, *Tales of the Hasidim*, II, pp. 140-1.
(21)   Psalm 71:9.
(22)   Buber, *Hasidism and Modern Man*, p. 191.
(23)   Buber, *Ten Rungs: Hasidic Sayings*, NY: Schocken, 1947, p. 51.
(24)   Talmud, Yevamot 63B.
(25)   Rabbi Shim ben Elazar in Avot deRabbi Nathan, chap. 41.

VII. Humor, Laughter and Originality

Rabbi Pinhas said: "All joys hail from paradise, and jests too, provided they are uttered in true joy."[26]

"Were it not for the crazies (*m'shuga-im*), the world could not exist."[27]

"The real voyage of discovery consists not in seeking new landscapes, but in having new eyes."[28] For example, on Purim there is a command to be intoxicated to the point that one cannot distinguish between "Cursed be Haman and blessed be Mordecai." (*Ad-lo-yada*). Frivolity. Simchat Torah – letting go, spontaneity.

VIII. Awe, wonder, ineffable, mystery, mystic insight

1. "The greatest insights happen to us in moments of awe."[29]
2. Maslow – peak experiences.
3. Psalms, Siddur, kabbalah, kavanah (interiority), Hasidism.

God says to humans as God said to Moses: "Put off thy shoes from off thy feet" – put off the habitual which encloses your foot and you will recognize that the place on which you happen to be standing at this moment is holy ground, for "there is no rung of being on which we cannot find the holiness of God everywhere and at all times."[30]

IX. Originality

A Hasid said to the maggid of Zlotchov: "We are told, 'Everyone in Israel is duty bound to say: When will my work approach the works of my fathers, Abraham, Isaac and Jacob?'"

How are we to understand this? How could we ever venture to think that we could do what our fathers did?

The rabbi expounded: "Just as our fathers found new ways of serving, each a new service according to his character: one the service of love, the other that of stern justice, the third that of beauty, so each of us in his own way shall devise something new in the light of teachings and of service, and do what has

---

(26) Buber, *Tales of the Hasidim* I,135.
(27) Maimonides, *Shemoneh Perakim*.
(28) Marcel Proust (cf. Heschel, "The Pious Man," *Man Is Not Alone*).
(29) Heschel, *God in Search of Man*, p. 78.
(30) Buber, *Ten Rungs*, p. 15.

not yet been done."[31]

X. Creativity. Mental Health and Judaism

1) Creativity as an Index of Personality Health: Creativity as developing latent potential Creativity and Self-actualization.

2) Creativity as the curative force in psychotherapy: God the Creator – paradigm of creativity.
- A human's highest calling – Imitatio Dei.
- Creativity as the ultimate purpose.
- The person as God's partner in creation.

3) The Jewish view of the World as Unfinished.
- The highest task of life – to complete creation. (Talmudic and Hasidic sources on the role of creativity and the person as Partner with God in creation.)

4) A Jewish model for creativity: Midrash.
- The process of searching for truth.
- Contemporizing literature and history.
- Midrash as a creative source for interpretation of classical texts.
- Samples of creative Midrash.

5) Awe and mysticism as experiencing life creatively.
- Effective prayer requires creativity.
- Religion, poetry and creativity.
- Creativity as a source for peak experience.

6) Creativity and the healthy personality.
- Qualities of health and creativity: openness, flexibility, originality, humor.
- Health as an expression of one's true self.
- Creativity, Sensuality and Sexuality.

7) Visualization as Creativity as a tool for fostering healing and wholeness.
- Imagination – a Jewish quality.
- Faith and Imagery.
- Jewish Images, past and present.
- Images, role models, and visualization.

---

(31)   Buber, *Hasidism and Modern Man*, p. 139.

Part II
People

| 9 |

Rabbi Abraham Joshua Heschel, My Teacher

Rabbi Abraham Joshua Heschel, a spiritual giant of the twentieth century, died on the 18th of Tevet in 1972.

Abba Eban (1915-2002), the late Israeli ambassador to the US, and Israel's foreign minister, defined this generation as one of Hasidim, disciples, seeking a rebbe, a master. For many Jews and Christians, Rabbi Heschel was that master.

During January we read in the Torah the story of the Jewish People's struggle to emerge from slavery to freedom. The mass exodus of Jews in the former Soviet Union (over one million) began with the clarion call from Rabbi Heschel in the 1960s, not to forget our imprisoned people behind the Iron Curtain. But Heschel's vision was broad, and his concern for all God's children extended to African Americans, prompting him to march with Rev. Martin Luther King, Jr., in Selma, when he famously said "My feet are praying," and to work together with Dr. King in other ways to free Blacks from omnipresent, pernicious racism in our society. Rabbi Heschel also worked with protesters in the anti-Vietnam struggle. His strong and pure voice resounded throughout America and the Jewish and general world.

Rabbi Abraham Heschel, presenting Judaism and World Peace award to Dr. Martin Luther King, Jr., 1965.

Rabbi Heschel was caught up by the passion of the biblical prophets whose face he possessed with his compassionate features and his head of rich white hair, Heschel himself looked like a prophet from Biblical days. He sought the redemption of human society, the betterment of the human lot, and the elevation of the human soul. Not long before his death in December 1972, Heschel said, "I've written a book on the [biblical] Prophets ... and the book has changed my life. Because early in my life my great love was for learning, studying. And the place where I preferred to live was my study and books and writing and thinking. I've learned from the prophets that I have to be involved in the affairs of man, in the affairs of suffering man."

Heschel said, "My heart is sick when I think of the anguish and the sighs, of the quiet tears shed in the nights in the overcrowded dwellings, of the pangs of despair, of the cup of humiliation that is running over. When blood is shed, human eyes see red, when a heart is crushed, it is only God who shares the pain."

Professor Heschel was a passionate Zionist. He wrote, "With the establishment of the State of Israel , the whole Jewish world was filled with light. But we have still not learned how to use that light." His love of Israel prompted him to write a moving book on Israel and its rebirth, *Israel: An Echo of Eternity.* And when it was necessary to speak up for Israel, or Soviet Jewry, or other Jewish causes, that was his priority. He never saw a conflict between Jewish concerns and universal causes, but he knew that he was a Jew, and tended his own garden before turning to try to heal the world.

When I had the privilege of having Professor Heschel as my teacher in theology at the Jewish Theological Seminary, and he was absent from class for several weeks, we students later found out that he had been called to Rome to consult with Pope John 23rd. The Vatican II Council, at that time, helped bring the Church to the twentieth century. Among other important progressive steps, the Church eliminated the phrase "the perfidious Jews" updating the Catholic Mass. It was Heschel's persuasiveness at the time that led to this important and necessary change. At that time the Pope changed the phrase about insisting that Jews convert to Christianity. Heschel told the Pope and his assistants that if he had the choice of converting or going to Auschwitz, he would choose the latter.

His influence on the Catholic world and the rest of humanity covered the planet.

The Talmud says that when a great soul is lost, everyone is considered family (*Hakham she-met hakol k'rovav*). The world was orphaned when Rabbi Heschel was untimely taken from us, at age sixty-five, at the height of his intellectual powers. He was a gifted expositor of our faith, our voice to the world, an authentic, soaring voice and a poetic soul, who appears once in a century. His words, but even more, his life, as a scholar, spiritual leader and model Jew and human being, will live on to inspire us.

Rabbi Heschel was a major figure in American political life and world affairs. His influence with American Presidents, the Pope, and other international figures emerged from his stature as a world-renowned scholar of Jewish theology, philosophy and Hebrew literature.

One of Heschel's major works of theology is titled *God in Search of Man*. (He surely would have used more gender-sensitive language had he lived in our generation). In his book he claimed that religion is not a psychological need of humans, but rather a need of God. The Bible (Tanakh) is not theology, but Divine anthropology. Heschel's poetic language is audacious, hyperbolic, but authentic and instructive. Students of Aristotelian scholasticism spoke of God as the Unmoved Mover. Heschel wrote of God as the Most Moved Mover. He wrote of the pathos that God feels in the events of the universe created by God.

In theological circles, Professor Heschel's approach is referred to as "depth theology." By this he meant that it is not sufficient to talk about God, or even to conceptualize God in abstract terms. Rather, what is needed is to experience the divine – to believe rather than just to discuss the content of belief. For others theology declares; for him theology evokes. For others theology is discussed in abstractions and generalizations. Heschel's depth theology places a premium on spontaneity and uniqueness. To him conceptual theology was necessary, but inadequate. It misses the mystery of the universe.

Mystery is one of the keys to understanding Rabbi Heschel's

thought. Among his important phrases are "the sense of the ineffable," and "radical amazement." One cannot take for granted the daily blessings of being alive, being part of God's universe. A pious person is shaken to the core every time the sun sets. Such a person is a poet of the spirit, and never tires of the beauty and holiness of our world.

Perhaps Heschel's best-known work is his book, *The Sabbath: Its Meaning for the Modern Man.* Heschel wrote of the importance of time. He called the Sabbath a "palace in time." The Sabbath is a time when we focus on the creation of the world, but also on the world of creation.

There is so much more to say, but how can one summarize a life's work in a brief column. Let Heschel speak for himself in these two brief passages:

"There is thus only one way to wisdom: awe. Forfeit your sense of awe, let your conceit diminish your ability to revere, and the universe becomes a marketplace for you. The loss of awe is the great block to insight. A return to reverence is the first prerequisite for a revival of wisdom, for the discovery of the world as an allusion to God. Wisdom comes from awe rather than from shrewdness. It is evoked not in moments of calculation but in moments of being in rapport with the mystery of reality."

On prayer he wrote:

"Those who run precipitately through the liturgy, rushing in and out of the prayer-texts, as if the task were to cover a maximum of space in a minimum of time, will derive little from worship. To be able to pray is to know how to stand still and to dwell upon a word."

Dr. Heschel spoke at a White House Conference on Aging in 1961. There he said:

"Old age is a major challenge to the inner life; it takes both wisdom and strength not to succumb to it."

In terms of manpower he (the aged) is a liability, a burden, a drain on our resources. Conditioned as a machine for making and spending money, with all other relationships depending upon its efficiency, the moment the machine is out of order and beyond repair, one begins to feel like a ghost without a sense of reality."

Rabbi Heschel raised our spirits when he said, "There is no human being who does not carry a treasure in his soul; a moment of insight, a memory of love, a dream of excellence, a call to worship. We must seek ways to overcome the traumatic fear of being old; have prejudice, discrimination against those advanced in years ... Being old is not necessarily the same as being stale ... Old men need a vision, not only recreation. Old men need a dream, not only a memory."

In a televised program, a few weeks before he died, Carl Stern interviewed Professor Heschel, and in the closing statement, Stern asked him if he had anything to say to the youth of this generation. Heschel replied:

"Remember that there is a meaning beyond absurdity ... that every little deed counts, that every word has power, and that we can all do our share to redeem the world. ... And above all, remember that the meaning of life is to build a life as if it were a work of art."

As years pass, we recognize more and more how much Rabbi Heschel contributed to the world. New scholars and teachers can be trained, but how can a pious soul be replaced? He died on Shabbat, the Shabbat of Parashat Vayehi, which means "And he lived." Rabbi Heschel gave Judaism and the Jewish People new life, with his deeds and his words.

His memory will forever be a blessing.

| 10 |

Rabbi Abraham Isaac Kook, Model Rabbinic Leader

Rav Kook, as he is known, is considered the leading rabbi of the twentieth century. Let's start with his biography, and then we'll discuss his philosophy and his major accomplishments.

Rav Kook was an early pioneer of traditional Zionism. He was a creative thinker, whose ideas resonate to this day. His impact on the Yishuv (Jewish settlement in Palestine) remains innovative and worthy of study.

Rav Kook was born in 1865, in Grieva, a small province in northwest Russia. At his Brit Milah his mother gave him a yarmulka made from the cloak of one of his pious ancestors. Abraham was born into a long line of rabbis, who were kohanim. As a youngster he took the yarmulka to bed, as children do. It was his "security blanket."

Rav Abraham Isaac Kook.

By age four he was already studying the Bible. Since he was a kohen he began with Sefer Vayikra. His parents spoke Hebrew at home, which was extremely unusual. Most Jews in that generation spoke either Russian or Yiddish. Hebrew was considered "*Leshon ha'kodesh*," and reserved for study and prayer. Here we have an early indication of welding the old with the new.

At age seven he began the study of the Talmud. At a very early age, he acquired a reputation of an "*Illui*" (a genius). He was fortunate to be blessed with a photographic memory. He was constantly aware of being a kohen, and was ready to resume offering sacrifices if the Messiah came and the holy

Temple in Jerusalem were restored. Eretz Yisrael may have been far off in space, but not in mind. The ultimate Redemption and the arrival of the Messiah was a real dream, for which they hoped every day. Among the games he played as a child was "Marching to *Eretz Yisrael*".

At age fifteen, his family decided that he had learned all he could in Grieva. Thus, he was sent to Lutzin, where students were welcomed with warm hospitality. From the early hours in the morning he sat in the Yeshivah, studying all day. Often he studied into the early hours of the dawn.

In the decade of the 1880s there were terrible pogroms, and Jews began to think more seriously of going to Eretz Yisrael. Small groups such as *Hibat Zion* mushroomed. It was dangerous to travel because of bandits on the roads, and diseases like malaria in Eretz Yisrael. Letters from family who had already settled in Eretz Yisrael wrote about the dangers facing those who had already traveled there.

The Kook family had learned of the *Musar* (Ethics) movement founded by Rabbi Israel Salanter of Kovno, Lithuania (1810-1883), and they moved to be closer to him. There Abraham pored over the many books of morality and ethics, which became an important part of his philosophy in later years.

The next step in young Abraham's education took place at age eighteen, when he moved to the famous center of learning in Eastern Europe, Volozhin, in the Minsk region of Belarus, where a Yeshivah was established around 1803 by Rabbi Hayyim Volozhiner, a student of the famed Vilna Gaon, Rabbi Elijah ben Solomon Zalman (1720-1797).

The Dean of the Yeshivah, Rabbi Naftali Zvi Yehudah Berlin[1], already had heard of the young *Ilui*, Abraham Isaac (Avraham Yitzhak). At the Yeshivah some of the students argued with Avraham because he wanted to speak in Hebrew, while others insisted on reserving Hebrew for holy matters. How could he turn a sacred vessel into a secular instrument, they contended. Abraham Isaac argued that every day must be sanctified and hallowed, and speaking Hebrew would help accomplish that. In addition, he reminded them that in the days of the Bible, people spoke Hebrew, and now in Eretz Yisrael Hebrew was spoken

(1)   Known as the "Netziv," the acronym of his name, 1816-1893.

more and more. Jews all over Russia were longing for a return to a normal life as a nation, to cast off the shackles of the Exile. We too, said Abraham, should be an important part of the new movement of Redemption.

"So why can't we also speak Hebrew?" Abraham told his friends that speaking Hebrew was the wave of the future, the beginning of the Redemption of the Jewish People. His friends argued that we should not force the hand of God. God will bring the Redemption, when He is ready, it is not up to us to do it. Abraham's reply was that God will redeem us when we are ready, when we return to the Land of our ancestors, and speak the language of the Bible.

Rabbi Berlin looked favorably on the young Zionist pioneers, who were settling the Land. He said that God will help our youth, who may not be religious, to find values in Torah. As the Talmud teaches, the very air of Eretz Yisrael purifies and brings wisdom to all who live there. On the other side, some very strict rabbis scorned the Zionist youth because they neglected reciting prayers and observing the rules of the Sabbath. While Abraham was sympathetic and patient with the young people, the more strict rabbis called them blasphemers, who did not care for the holy tradition.

After some time, Abraham Isaac matured and received rabbinic ordination. He married and moved to Ponivesh, where his father-in-law was known as a great rabbinic scholar. There he taught, lectured, studied, and filled the role of one of the rabbis. There he came into contact with another important influence in his life, Rabbi Israel Meir of Radin, known as the "Hafetz Hayyim," from the name of his most famous book. Both men were kohanim, and they studied together the law of kehunah (priesthood). Then Rav Kook was persuaded to serve as the only rabbi in a new community, Zoimel. He remained there with his wife for six years.

In Zoimel, Rav Kook faced a difficult problem. There was a terrible epidemic of a serious disease, cholera. The holy day of fasting, Yom Kippur, was coming soon, and Rav Kook realized that if people did not eat or drink, as Jewish law required, they would be weak and would likely contract the disease. He made a courageous decision. He stood on the pulpit of the synagogue on Yom Kippur morning, pronounced the *motzee*, the prayer before breaking bread, and took a bite of bread. He made an official rabbinic pronouncement, telling the congregation that they must eat, to strengthen themselves and prevent them from contracting cholera. He explained that preventing disease and preventing serious illness and death are more important in Jewish law than fasting on Yom Kippur. The law is based on a verse in the biblical Book of Leviticus (18:5) – "and you shall live by them" (the laws), and the commentators explain and add "and not die by them").

Still later Rabbi Kook was persuaded to move to another community, Boisk, in Latvia. There he encountered the new movement of "*Haskalah*," (Enlightenment). It had spread through Western Europe, and now made its way to Eastern Europe. Religious Jews were opposed to many of the ideas of the new movement, fearing that the study of secular subjects, such as philosophy, foreign literature and science,. The supporters of *Haskalah* studied the Hebrew language, along with other tongues, they loved the Land, but they did not observe the traditional rituals, such as kashrut, Shabbat and holidays.

Rav Kook's view was more moderate. He taught that one should not fear having the Torah competing with other learning. The Torah, he taught, can stand up for itself, and can compete successfully with the wisdom of other cultures. He was willing to read the books of foreign philosophers. His view was that knowledge from many sources was helpful in understanding God's universe. They helped him, he said, to become more religious, more devoted to his own religion.

After serving in Boisk for several years, he announced to his congregation that he had decided to fulfill his life's dream, going up to live in the Land of Israel.

Many people pleaded with him not to go. There were hundreds of thousands of Jews in Russia, while in Eretz Yisrael there were only a small number of pioneers. Yet, he felt that now at age thirty-nine it was now or never. He had accepted an offer to become the rabbi of the city of Jaffa.

When he arrived in Jaffa, he pronounced the well-known prayer, "...*she-he-heyanu*... – Blessed are You, Holy One, who has kept us in life, sustained us, and enabled us to reach this sacred moment." He bent down and kissed the holy soil, with enormous joy and satisfaction in his heart. It is said that when he spotted a cow, he approached it, kissed it, and screamed, "An Eretz-Yisrael-ish kuh" (cow).

In Jaffa he immediately plunged into new conflicts between different groups of Jews: Ashkenazim and Sephardim, Hasidim and Mitnagdim, elderly pious students and young pioneers.

Rav Kook saw his role as conciliator, between tradition and modernity, East and West, pious and rebellious.

In June 1914, Rav Kook was invited to address a group of traditional rabbis called Agudat Yisrael, who were meeting in Germany. He and his wife traveled there for a two-week stay. As events happened, they remained for five years, until the end of the First World War. As Russian citizens, they were interned in Germany. Several rabbis in Berlin knew of Rav Kook, and arranged to have him and his wife freed. On June 15, they were able to cross the German border to Geneva, Switzerland. A pious Jew in a small town in Switzerland, Saint Gallen, named Abraham Kimchi, arranged a place for them to live until the end of the War.

Rav Kook's life during these quiet years was extremely important for him. It gave him time for study, meditation and prayer. In this tranquil atmosphere Rav Kook wrote some of his most moving essays and philosophical works.

In 1916, he received an invitation from a congregation in London, Machzeekay HaDat. While it was a safe refuge during the War, he was not completely happy living in exile. At the end of every letter, he signed his name, "Rabbi Abraham Isaac Hakohen Kook, the Rabbi of Jaffa, and now in London."

One fortunate aspect of Rav Kook's stay in London was his ability to be involved in Zionist affairs. Chaim Weizmann, a biochemist and Zionist leader (1874-1952), who was a professor in the chemistry department of the University of Manchester, had been working to persuade the British government to support the idea of a Jewish homeland in Eretz Yisrael. Ironically the only Jewish member of the British Cabinet, Lord Edwin Montague, was opposed to the idea, arguing that "We Jews are loyal to England."

Rav Kook circulated a letter which was read in every

synagogue in London, urging support for the British government to make a statement in support of the Jewish homeland. The influence of Weizmann and Rav Kook helped move the idea forward, and on November 2, 1917, Foreign Secretary Arthur Balfour called Weizmann and Rav Kook to his office with the good news. His famous "Balfour Declaration" announced British support for the establishment of a "national home for the Jewish People" in Palestine (Palestine was the name the Romans gave to the area two thousand years before).

After the War, in 1919, Rav Kook returned to Eretz Yisrael. This time it was not to Jaffa, but to the holy city of Jerusalem, where he was invited to become the Chief Rabbi. The year before, the British had taken the entire area from the Ottoman Empire, and Sir Herbert Samuel was appointed by the British government to be High Commissioner of Palestine. Samuel wanted each religious group to handle its own affairs, such as marriage, divorce, personal status, etc. He asked Rav Kook to be the rabbi of the entire Jewish community, and become Chief Rabbi of Eretz Yisrael. Thus, in 1921, Rav Kook became the first Chief Rabbi, until his death in 1935.

During his fourteen years as Chief Rabbi he became beloved by the entire Jewish community. When some of the more strict rabbis argued with him about his acceptance of young pioneers who claimed to be atheists, and were destroying Judaism, Rav Kook replied with a strong answer. He explained that when the holy Temple was being built in Jerusalem, the only person permitted to enter the Holy of Holies, the inner sanctum of the Temple complex, was the high priest on Yom Kippur. On that one supremely holiest day of the year, no one but the kohen gadol could enter. Yet, when there was need of repair, any workman could enter, in simple, shabby clothing, to do the work.

"I view these young pioneers," explained Rav Kook, "as the workers of our new Temple, the holy land, who labor with devotion, building our renewed nation. They are motivated by a divine spark, and we must encourage them, not criticize them."

"Do not say they lack piety," he continued. "Every Jew has the spark of the Divine within. If they are temporarily sidetracked, do not worry. Their true holy self will eventually emerge. Years of exile have influenced us. Pogroms and persecution have warped our nature. The free air of Eretz Yisrael will invigorate them and all of us. The Land has therapeutic quality."

There are many stories about Rav Kook's saintliness and persuasiveness.

Once a visitor from Denver, Colorado came to see him. He told Rav Kook how upset he was to meet so many non-religious Jews in the Holy Land. Seeming to ignore the remark, Rav Kook asked the visitor a question. "What kind of place is Denver? I heard that it is full of sick people with tuberculosis. It must be a very unhealthy city."

The visitor relied, "On the contrary. Because of the healing quality of the climate, people who are sick come here from all over the world to be healed." The visitor stood in silence, and thought, for a minute. Then his eyes were opened, and he understood the rabbi's point. The message came across to the visitor very powerfully.

Rav Kook taught many individuals and groups that simply living in Eretz Yisrael is a *mitzvah*. It was the first step to living a full religious life. He often signed his name on letters he wrote, "Rabbi Abraham Isaac Kook, Servant of a Holy People in a Holy Land."

His rabbinic colleagues argued with him: "Your love for these young pioneers is baseless love." His reply became famous: "Better baseless love than baseless hatred. (In Hebrew, better to have *Ahavat Hinam* rather than *Sinat Hinam*.) We need more unconditional love, love with no ulterior motive," he argued.

Rav Kook was very proud of his new home, despite its rough beginnings. He told his community not to look at our house while it's under construction, with builders abound in shabby and soiled garments. When the swamps are drained, the land irrigated, the mosquitos destroyed, and the enemy leaves us alone, we'll become a great nation.

The motto of Rav Kook became famous: *Hayashan yithadesh, ve-hehadash yitkadesh.* Even one who does not know Hebrew can hear the poetic alliteration in these words. And when one understands their meaning, it becomes even more powerful: "The old will be renewed and the new will become holy."

Soon after becoming Chief Rabbi he established a yeshivah, Mercaz HaRav, located in the Kiryat Moshe neighborhood in Jerusalem. The yeshivah has become the most prominent religious-Zionist yeshivah in the world and synonymous with Rabbi Kook's teachings. Students flocked to hear his lectures. In his yeshivah, he sought to blend modern approaches with the traditional. He wanted his students not only to study the holy books of the past, but also to create literature for the present and future.

Rav Kook was a prolific author. His commentary on the siddur is widely read. It is not a history of the prayers, but a meaningful explanation of how inspiring the thoughts are. In 1936, shortly after his death, a research foundation and publishing house was established – Mossad HaRav Kook, which still publishes his scores of books.

Rav Kook's brilliant mind was legendary. He read widely, including books on science and philosophy. When Albert Einstein visited Palestine, he met with Rav Kook. After an hour of discussion, Einstein's assistant told him that he had another appointment. "Never mind," answered the Nobel Prize scholar, "I do not want to be interrupted. Rabbi Kook is one of the few people in the world who understands my Theory of Relativity."

Rav Kook's love of Jewish mysticism was well known. One rabbi tells of visiting him one night at a very late hour. When he knocked and there was no answer, he pushed the door open slightly, and saw the Rav studying the holy mystical book, the Zohar. He later reported that he saw a streak of light emanating from the aging saint as he studied.

Another friend invited Rav Kook to walk with him to the synagogue for the evening prayers. Rav Kook asked him to wait a short while, explaining, "I am so much afire with the love of God, that if I go to the synagogue right now I will be consumed by fire. First I must take a walk and cool off."

Rav Kook died on the third day of the Hebrew month of Elul (September 1, 1935), the same date in the Hebrew calendar on which he arrived in Jerusalem to become Chief Rabbi. His funeral was attended by an estimated 20,000 mourners.

When he left this world, it was said of him, "We have lost the High Priest of the generation of Jewish Rebirth."

| 11 |

Ahad Ha'am – Cultural Nationalism

A had Ha'am was one of the foremost thinkers of the late nineteenth and early twentieth centuries. He was an essayist of high stature, and his writings are classics of modern Jewish life.

He was born Asher Ginzberg, but known primarily by his *nom de plume,* Ahad Ha'am (one of the people) (1856, Ukraine – 1927, Tel Aviv).

His father was a prosperous merchant, who forbade his son to study secular books. Ahad Ha'am was determined to expose himself to worldly culture, so he locked himself in his bedroom and immersed himself in literature of all kinds. He learned to read Russian from signs on store windows.

Ahad Ha'am.

He was married at age sixteen to a woman with an "illustrious pedigree."

At a young age he began to meet some of the leading intellectuals of the *Haskalah* (Enlightenment) movement. While no longer religiously observant himself, he was repelled by the anti-religiosity of the *maskilim* (followers of *Haskalah*). He maintained a warm feeling for Jewish tradition.

At age twenty-five, he was confronted with the "May Laws" of 1882, by Czar Alexander III of Russia, forcing Jews to live in crowded towns in the Pale of Settlement, followed by pogroms that destroyed thousands of Jewish homes and left thousands economically ruined. These terrible events motivated him to find some solutions for his fellow Jews.

Following years of thought and discussion, he wrote a letter that was published in a Hebrew newspaper, titled "Lo zeh Haderekh," ("This is not the Way"). In his letter he asked, "Why are the ideas of a national Jewish rebirth not spreading?" His answer was that people were appealing to their economic interests, and not to national sentiments. The task of those supporting the Zionist cause, such as the group called "*Hovevei Zion* – Lovers of Zion," was not to solve Jewish economic needs, but to strive towards the revival of the Jewish spirit. He signed his letter with his *nom de plume*, "Ahad Ha'am," to indicate that he was not a professional writer, just "a visitor in the tent of literature."

His revolutionary views on Zionism were met with strong controversy.

In 1889, a group was established to promote the new ideas offered by Ahad Ha'am. The new society, called *B'nai Moshe*, lasted for eight years. In 1891, he made his first voyage to Palestine. He spent three months visiting old ruins as well as new growing colonies. In 1893, he made another trip, remaining for six weeks.

After having made these visits, he was now prepared to promote his new ideas more widely. In 1895, he published a volume of essays in Hebrew, called "*Al Parashat Derakhim* – At the Crossroads". This turned out to be a crucial moment, since the first Zionist Congress took place two years later in 1897.

With the support of a wealthy Moscow merchant, in 1896 he launched a literary journal called *HaShiloah* The name was taken from a river mentioned in Isaiah 8:6, "The waters of Shiloaḥ flow slowly", alluding to the moderate stance of the paper. He advocated slow, steady progress, as opposed to many among the Zionists who favored a precipitous revolutionary movement to create a national Jewish state. His magazine became highly regarded, and greatly assisted in the revitalization of the Hebrew language.

Ahad Ha'am's main idea was opposed to that of Theodor Herzl, who called together major Jewish leaders for the First Zionist Congress in Basel, Switzerland in 1897. Herzl's desire was to set in motion the wheels toward creation of a Jewish state in Eretz Yisrael, to save Jews from persecution. Many in the Zionist Congress were highly excited about his plan. Ahad Ha'am, on the other hand, felt that it was more important to prepare the people culturally and spiritually, and the Jewish state would come after the people were more prepared. At the Congress he called himself "a mourner among the bridegrooms."

To Ahad Ha'am the purpose of Zionism was a moral one, "to liberate ourselves from inner slavery, from feelings of inferiority and to strengthen our national unity until Jews will be ready for a new life.... The salvation of Israel will come through prophets and not through diplomats."

While Ahad Ha'am did not favor a formal national state in the short term, he was in favor of Jews settling in the Land. The settlers would create a new culture and an indigenous Jewish atmosphere.

> "This Jewish settlement will become in the course of time the center of the nation, wherein its spirit will find pure expression and develop in all its aspects to the highest degree of perfection.... Later, at a favorable moment the people there may be ready to establish a State, one which will be not merely a State of Jews, but a truly Jewish State."

In 1899, Ahad Ha'am again traveled to Palestine, and that year he published two more volumes of "At the Crossroads." Later, in 1908, he accepted a position with the Wissotzky Tea Company in London, and gave up his editorship of *HaShiloah*. He spent the next fourteen years in London with his wife and two children.

In 1914, when he released the fourth and final volume of "At the Crossroads", his literary career came to an end. His daughter Rachel had married a non-Jew, which affected him deeply. He had written strongly against intermarriage, describing it as a blow to Jewish survival.

At the same time, he became ill with heart disease and never fully recovered. In 1921, he decided to settle in Tel Aviv with his wife and son. He worked on collecting and editing his correspondence of some 1,700 letters. The material was published in six volumes from 1923 to 1925.

In 1926, the world celebrated his seventieth birthday. A year later he died and was buried in the old cemetery of Tel Aviv.

Philosophy

Ahad Ha'am saw the political and material bases of nationalism as subordinate to the role of the spiritual and moral foundations.

In his essay "The Law of the Heart", he claimed that the Jewish People relied in the past two thousand years too much on the written word, and not enough on creative expression. "Only in that way," he wrote, "can the Jewish soul be freed from its shackles and regain contact with the road stream of human life, without having to pay for its freedom by the sacrifice of its individuality."

He believed there are three basic values which reflect the soul of the Jewish People, and helped the Jews survive.

First, its language.

The Hebrew language bears the imprint of the spirit of our people. A national language is one in which the spiritual treasures of the nation have been written. Only the Hebrew language carried the high ideals of the chain of generations, expressing its sacred feelings, its joys and sorrows.

Second, its religion.

Although not ritually observant personally, he saw in the traditions great importance in the life of our people: its customs and rituals are our national symbols. He attended synagogue periodically, recited the mourner's kaddish for his parents on a regular basis, and never traveled on Jewish holidays.

Third, Jewish identity.

When a leading French Jew urged Eastern Europeans to become emancipated from Jewish ceremonial laws like the Sabbath and dietary laws, he said that these institutions have been "sanctified by the blood of our people, and have preserved it for thousands of years from spiritual degeneration."

When someone suggested that the Sabbath was a useless institution, he replied, "One who feels a true bond with the life of his people cannot visualize the existence of the Jewish People without Queen Sabbath." Further he said, famously, "More than the Jewish People observed the Sabbath, the Sabbath preserved the Jewish People."

Jewish thinkers debated the merits of Theodor Herzl's vision of creating a Jewish state, and Ahad Ha'am's dream of cultural Zionism preceding and preparing for the Jewish state, for many years. In the end, the world situation leaned toward Herzl's vision. The pogroms of the 1930s in Palestine, the Second World War and the Holocaust all created the necessity of following Herzl's political Zionism. The physical emergency of assisting persecuted Jews necessitated the creation of a Jewish state in Eretz Yisrael.

Nevertheless, much was learned by the vision of Ahad Ha'am. His stress on the cultural and religious aspects of Jewish life, in the Diaspora and in the State of Israel, were lessons that helped the entire Jewish People understand that Israel must not become only a state of Jews, but also a Jewish state.

For his significant contribution toward strengthening Jewish culture, many cities in the State of Israel are named after Ahad Ha'Am.

For all his influence on the people of Israel, we owe a great debt to a great thinker, and a loyal son of our people.

| 12 |

Qualities of the Person of Tomorrow

I write this essay with great trepidation. A wise person once said that predictions and prophecy are daring and audacious, especially when they are about the future. But with a proper measure of chutzpah, I will give it a try.

First a general statement.

The qualities our society lacks today are female qualities. If we want to create a society that is better than today's, it will have to be a society with qualities that most males do not possess. Since women are more than fifty percent of the US population, the new society will obviously be much different in many significant ways than today's.

First, it is my hope that the person of tomorrow will be open-minded and s/he will be open to see the world in new ways, and be able to accept new ideas.

A phrase I heard recently describes the majority of males in today's world: psychosclerosis. We all know what atherosclerosis is – hardening of the arteries. Psychosclerosis is hardening of the mind, being impervious to new thoughts, new ideas.

The French philosopher Emile Chartier said that there is nothing as dangerous as an idea when it is the only one you have. The more light you admit to the pupil of the eyes of people afraid of something new, the narrower the pupil becomes.

A story will illustrate my point. A group of European rabbis met to discuss words of Torah. Each rabbi delivered an interpretation of a verse that he received from his distinguished ancestors. One young scholar had no scholarly ancestors, and said to his colleagues: "My masters, my father was a baker. He taught me that only fresh bread is appetizing, and that is why I must avoid the stale. This can also apply to learning." With those remarks, he sat down.

The next quality of the person of tomorrow is authenticity.

In Talmudic tradition there is a well-known principle which says that a person should be "*tokho k'varo,*" that a person should be the same inside and outside. In other words, one should say and do that which is part of her/him, not to be deceitful, duplicitous or hypocritical. One should not engage in double-talk, but rather be sincere and transparent.

Another Hebrew phrase resembling the above principle is *"ehad bapeh v'ehad balev,"* namely that what is in one's heart should be the same as what comes out of one's mouth. This means that one should be honest to one's spouse, to one's children, to one's friends, and most of all, to oneself. The Hasidic master Rabbi Simhah Bunam[1] taught that the worst liar is the one who lies to himself.

The next quality of the person of tomorrow, as I envision the future, is that the person has a desire for intimacy.

Such an individual will care deeply about communication, which should be direct, clear and honest. That person will feel comfortable with hugs and fraternal physical contact, and not be afraid that it would be misinterpreted as gay or foolish.

Sharing feelings and emotions will be natural to someone close, and with whom one has a warm relationship. Sharing feelings include times of sadness, grief, fear, joy, hope, and triumph.

In Psalms[2] we read, "Enlarge the site of your tent, and extend the size of your dwelling." This can mean, metaphorically, deepen your relationships.

The Talmudic tractate Pirke Avot (1:6) teaches "Acquire a friend..." How should this be done? Eat with him, read together with him, study with him, reveal your secrets to him.

The next quality of a person of tomorrow is that s/he is ready to take risks.

A person should be willing to stick one's neck out, try new things, be open to new experiences.

An old joke states that when Adam and Eve were leaving the Garden of Eden, Adam said to Eve, "We're living in an age of transition." The fact is that today's world is filled with transitions. Many more people are changing jobs, moving to new locations, accepting new challenges, learning new methods and ideas.

(1) 1765-1827, Poland.
(2) Isaiah 54:2.

One who insists on living solely in the world of our fathers and mothers will rarely make progress. The person of tomorrow will not have the attitude of the caterpillar that looked at a butterfly and said, "You'll never find me flying around in one of those crazy things."

James B. Conant, president of Harvard University 1933-1953, is said to have kept a model of a turtle on his desk with the inscription, "Consider the turtle. He makes progress only when he sticks his neck out."

The next quality of the person of tomorrow will be that the person truly and deeply cares. The person will care about fellow travelers on spaceship earth. Such caring extends to people, regardless of color, creed, religion, ideology, etc.

Jewish tradition has an all-encompassing word for deep caring: *Hesed*. *Hesed* includes steadfast, constant love. Love for others, love for family, friends, neighborhood, the planet, the poor, the stranger and the homeless. Such caring is best when it is gentle, often subtle, and nonjudgmental.

In the biblical book of Psalms (89:3), we read "God's *hesed* (lovingkindness) lasts forever."

The Talmud reminds us that the Torah begins and ends with *hesed*. In the beginning of the Torah, we read of God clothing Adam and Eve. At the end of the Torah, we read of the burial of Moses[3].

The late Leo Buscaglia, professor at the University of Southern California, was asked to offer a topic for a special lecture. He replied that his lecture would be on "Love." He was told that this topic was unacceptable. So he changed the topic and offered this one: "Positive Affect as a Determinant of Behavior." This topic was acceptable.

People of tomorrow understand that love is the best way to celebrate life.

Finally, the person of tomorrow will be a seeker.

A seeker tries to find meaning and purpose in life that is greater than oneself. She desires to live a life of inner tranquility. Her models are people like Mahatma Gandhi, Martin Luther King Jr., Teilhard de Chardin, Henry David Thoreau, Abraham Joshua Heschel, Rosa Parks, Mother Teresa, Oprah

---

(3)   Tractate Sota 14A.

Winfrey, Maya Angelou, Winston Churchill, Eleanor Roosevelt, Elie Wiesel.

I close with the eloquent challenge of one searcher, the poet James Kavanaugh:

"I am one of the searchers. There are, I believe, millions of us. We are not unhappy, but neither are we really content. We continue to explore life, hoping to uncover its ultimate secret. We continue to explore ourselves, hoping to understand. We like to walk along the beach, we are drawn by the ocean, taken by its power, its unceasing motion, its mystery and unspeakable beauty. We like forests and mountains, deserts and hidden rivers, and the lonely cities as well. Our sadness is as much a part of our lives as is our laughter. To share our sadness with one we love is perhaps as great a joy as we can know – unless it be to share our laughter.

"We searchers are ambitious only for life itself, for everything beautiful it can provide. Most of all, we love and want to be loved. We want to live in a relationship that will not impede our wandering, nor prevent our search, nor lock us in prison walls; that will take us for what little we have to give. We do not want to prove ourselves to another or compete for love. For wanderers, dreamers, and lovers, for lonely men and women who dare to ask of life everything good and beautiful. It is for those who are too gentle to live among wolves."

| 13 |

My Visit with Ashley Montagu

The Township of Princeton New Jersey was chock full of brilliant scholars, authors, professors, writers and a wide variety of intellectuals.

As rabbi of the only formal synagogue in Princeton, I decided that once a month our congregation (The Jewish Center of Princeton) should invite many of these world-renowned authorities to our synagogue for what we called "Lunch and Learn."

People were invited to bring a dairy lunch and the congregation would provide drinks and dessert.

For the next several years there followed month after month a parade of highly accomplished intellectuals, who were invited to speak on their area of expertise. It was an amazing pantheon of

Rabbi Dov Peretz Elkins (L) with Ashley Montagu, 1996.

well-known scholars, unlike anything I know about in any other congregation in North America.

For purposes of this essay, I want to concentrate on the visit of Ashley Montagu (1905-1999). Montagu lived in a small house not far from the synagogue, and was a prime example of the kind of well-known intellectuals in our area.

Many of the speakers were members of our congregation, and Montagu was one of the few who was not a member. There was no requirement for our speakers to be Jewish, but Montagu was, in fact, born Jewish. He was born in London with the name Israel Ehrenberg. I am not aware of when and why Israel Ehrenberg became Ashley Montagu, but I can speculate, later in this essay.

I invited Montagu to speak at one of our Lunch-and-Learn meetings, and he happily agreed, with one condition. All the other speakers chose a topic, based on their area of expertise. Montagu's condition was that he would not be bound to any topic, but rather would be happy to participate in a "question and answer" session. In other words, the participants could ask whatever they wanted (presumably many had heard about his books, of which there were sixty in his lifetime, or even read some of his voluminous writings), and he would reply. That suggestion was heartily accepted if it would make it possible for Ashley Montagu to be our guest for an hour or so of dialog.

His visit took place on June 13, 1995 (four years before his death). He asked to be picked up at his home, to which I gladly agreed, but in addition, I asked if I might arrive an hour early and chat with him. He agreed, and this essay is based on both my private meeting in his living room, and the Lunch-and-Learn session that followed.

It is important to note that what I now write is based on the scribbly notes I took during our living-room conversation, plus a column which I published in the synagogue bulletin a few weeks later.

Unfortunately, my hand-written notes, tucked away in a file for the past twenty-five years, are in many places illegible. But I am doing my best to read them and pass on the information I wrote about.

The first event during our personal meeting was his telling me that I should uncross my legs and ankles. He explained that he had taught anatomy in a medical school, hence this advice. (I have no idea how accurate this advice was medically, but I have tried over the years to follow it). He argued that such an anatomical position could cause harm to the heart.

Most of our conversation in his living room was based on my interest in his Jewish background. Naturally I wanted to find out if being a Jew was in any way significant to him, or if Judaism had influenced him at all, especially during his early years.

His discussion of his Jewishness reflected his ambivalence toward his Jewish background.

His parents, he said, were typical "high holiday synagogue goers." Even so, being Jewish had been very important to him, adding that most of his Jewish experiences were "not admirable." This would account for the fact that as an adult, and as a scientist (anthropology was his specialty) and as an academic, religion had little or no place in his life. He was, he said, an atheist.

He became bar mitzvah at age thirteen in London, as all the Jewish young boys did, and spent seven years in *"heder."* He learned to read and write Yiddish and Hebrew, and learned the musical tropes for the occasion.

His mother had come from a small shtetl near Odessa; his father had come from Lublin, Poland. His family arrived in London when he was sixteen years old. Today, he confessed, he could read neither of the two Jewish languages. He became a naturalized American citizen in 1940.

His parents, he told me, spoke Yiddish to each other, and often sang Yiddish songs.

When he ventured out of his Jewish neighborhood, the Christian boys would throw stones at him. When he asked his mother why they did that, she replied, "Because you are a Jew." Young Israel apparently experienced antisemitism on several occasions. Perhaps that is why he changed his name when he arrived in America.

His thoughts on being Jewish entered the conversation intermittently.

In 1923, he read Freud for the first time, and thought to himself, "this guy must be a Jew – the way he thinks."

If I am jumping around in this discussion, it is partly because my notes are not totally coherent, and because our conversation moved in and out of several themes.

His mother, he said, was illiterate. His father was a tailor, as most Jews at that time were confined to that trade. His mother was a good cook, and kept a kosher kitchen. He did not get along well with his father, who was physically rough. His mother, being a highly emotional creature, was very protective of him.

At one point in the conversation he pointed out, which I was ecstatic to hear, that he owes a great deal to his Jewish background. He enjoyed reading Abraham Joshua Heschel's *The Earth is the Lord's*, a lyrical account of Jewish life in Eastern Europe in the early twentieth century and before.

Among his friends were Erich Fromm (1900-1980), the famous psychoanalyst and philosopher, and Gordon Allport (1897-1967), a well-known psychologist, famous as the author of *The Nature of Prejudice.*

During a visit to Israel he was very impressed with how the country brought the deserts back to life. Many of his friends moved to Israel.

When asked what profession he would choose, he said a psychologist.

"Oh, you mean a doctor of fools", was the reply.

Regarding his personal beliefs, he said he did not believe that God is love; rather that love is God.[1]

His remarks were not without humor. He said that he felt his own children (he had three children, four grandchildren and two great-grandchildren) should have the experience of being part of a religious institution, and for a while his family were members of a Unitarian Church. And the only time he heard the word "Jesus" was when the janitor fell down the steps. The members of the church, he thought, were pagans, but were very good human beings. One does not need to celebrate or practice anything in a group, though he considered it important to be a member of humanity. If someone belongs to a group other than yours, they don't measure up.

He was opposed to nationalism; it's just another word for racism.

The principle that one should "love your neighbor as yourself" did not please him. One should love others more than you love yourself.

When we met, in 1995, he was ninety-one years old, and appeared to be in excellent health. He told me that one may grow older, but should never grow old. The body gets older, but the spirit never grows old.

I turn next to what I wrote about Montagu's visit to our congregation, and the points he made during the "question and answer" period. Here are some bon mots he expressed during that enjoyable interchange:
- I am a scientist, and a scientist believes in proof without

(1) Not sure what he meant by that comment.

certainty. Most people, on the other hand, believe in certainty without proof.

- The Egyptians said that God couldn't be everywhere, so he created mothers. This is accurate, since mothers give love, as God does. Love is God and God is love.
- While growing up and observing the way my parents treated me, I wondered if they were ever children. Most adults are deteriorated children.
- Our community lacks the intimacy and love of the shtetl. I learned more about Jewish culture, and was moved more, from the songs of the shtetl than from reading any book.
- When a question was asked which the speaker could not hear clearly, he commented: As you get older, other people's voices become softer.
- Women are superior to men. Any woman who wants to act like a man lacks ambition.
- Being famous means being known by many people who don't know you.
- Our leaders in Congress are crooks and many are insane. Insanity means you can't manage your own affairs.
- My books have become classics. A classic is a book that is unread or out-of-print.
- We humans are the only rational creatures who behave irrationally. We justify our irrational behavior by saying that "We've always done it that way."
- The definition of love: the communication to another of one's profound interest in their welfare by demonstrative acts.
- When you are unloved you seek power by running for office.
- We are the most self-destructive species on earth. During the last war 200 million people died. You blow the bugle, and people go to war.
- Science is a false messiah. It created nuclear weapons.
- A value is something that contributes to human welfare.
- When I read Freud it was obvious to me that he was a Jew, because he understood, through Talmudic reasoning, that something can be both A **and** B. Things

can contradict one another (i.e., love-hate).

- Homosexuals are people who had unloving fathers. They are afraid to love people of the opposite sex. This was discovered fifty years ago by George Henry in his book, *Sex Variants.*

- When asked how do we spread love and change our terrible world, the speaker answered: When we find the answer, it will be simple. There ought to be a sign over every laboratory: "When the problem will be solved, it will be found to be simple."

- When I was young I wanted to be a psychoanalyst, which I later learned is the study of the id by the odd. A psychoanalyst is a non-swimmer acting like a lifeguard.

These are the final lines of the column I wrote a few weeks following Montagu's visit:

In the car on the way home he told me that a Japanese scholar is publishing a book titled *The Wit and Wisdom of Ashley Montagu.* I hope it's translated into English very soon.

I don't know if such a book was ever published, but if not, it's surely a shame.

In sum, I hope I have given a reasonably accurate report of my visit with Ashley Montagu (nee Israel Ehrenberg) and what I learned from this remarkable gentleman.

| 14 |

My Retreat with Henry David Thoreau

O f all the excellent courses in which I enrolled during my
four years at Temple University (1955-1959), the most
important course was omitted.

I was an English major, and took courses on a wide variety
of English writers, poets, essayists, and biographers, including
British romantics, early English greats such as Geoffrey Chaucer,
later authors such as Robert Browning, Charles Dickens, George
Eliot, John Milton, Emily Dickinson, and, of course, the Bard –
William Shakespeare. And other moderns such as James Joyce,
C.S. Lewis, E.E. Cummings, T.S. Eliot, Robert Frost, and countless
others.

So what did I miss? The American transcendentalists, Ralph
Waldo Emerson and Henry David Thoreau, and others.

Over the years I occupied myself with mainly Jewish, Hebrew
writers and literature. But I always had a hankering to go back
and fill in an indispensable lacuna.

The opportunity arose about twenty years later, when
someone described to me an opportunity not only to read some
of the transcendentalists, but to spend a week taking a deep
dive into the writings and life of Henry David Thoreau. Being
an independent workshop leader and lecturer, no longer at that
time holding a full-time position as rabbi of a congregation, I
jumped at the chance.

What was this once-in-a-lifetime opportunity? To spend a
five-day seminar at the home of those very transcendentalists,
Concord, Massachusetts, and attend a workshop led by the
world's foremost authority on Thoreau, Walter Harding
(1917-1996). Later Professor Harding wrote the magisterial
and definitive biography of Thoreau, *The Days of Henry David
Thoreau*, and other books on Thoreau. He founded the Thoreau
Society, and served as its president.

I quickly signed up, paid the modest tuition, and there being
no hotels near the Thoreau Lyceum in Concord, where the

lectures took place, I arranged to stay at the home of Mr. John Godding, at 59 Elm Street in Concord, previously arranged by the Thoreau Lyceum, which sponsored the workshop. I stayed there from Sunday July 6 to July 11, 1980.

Upon arrival I was given a professionally-produced booklet, "Guide to Concord" advertising the several points of interest in Concord, including Thoreau House, an exact reproduction of his Walden hut at the Thoreau Lyceum, Walden Pond, the site of Thoreau's cabin, and Sleepy Hollow Knoll, the resting place of Emerson, Thoreau, Hawthorne and the Alcotts.

The Guide proudly described Concord as "a charming New England town with many facts, incorporated in 1635, rich in history ... where early Patriots, forewarned by Paul Revere, faced the British Militia on April 19, 1775, and fired "the shot heard round the world". Later, stated the Guide, "during the 1800s, Concord became famous as the home of noted American authors – Ralph Waldo Emerson, Nathanial Hawthorne, Margaret Sidney, and Henry David Thoreau – who lived, thought, and wrote here."

By 1980, I had taken courses at Temple University (B.A.), Gratz College (Hebrew Teachers Diploma), The Jewish Theological Seminary (M.H.L. and rabbinic ordination), and had participated in dozens of workshops at Growth Centers around the country. In addition, I had completed coursework for a second master's degree with University Associates in the field of Human Relations Development. In all these years, and with all these courses and workshops under my belt, by the time these five days at Concord were completed, I felt as though I had just finished the most comprehensive, inspiring, enlightening course in my entire life.

Not only was Walter Harding an authoritative and effective educator and lecturer, but besides his mastery of, and passion for the subject matter, the structure of the course, which included daily field trips to all the spots connected to the life and writings of Thoreau, all these together made the experience superlative.

Thoreau and Judaism

Thoreau.

It is not my intention to review the entire contribution to world literature that Thoreau made, or rehearse the long list of reasons why I have for so long considered Thoreau one of my greatest heroes. I hasten to add that at least one authority on the great thinkers of the Western world considers Thoreau's masterpiece, *Walden*, "one of the greatest books in world literature." The poet Robert Frost wrote of *Walden*, "In one book ... he surpasses everything we have had in America."

What I will write in the rest of this essay, will be that some of the many ideas contained in Thoreau's oeuvre, and relate to the concepts which I believe jive with time-honored ideas conceived in the Jewish tradition

Henry David Thoreau (1817-1862) is known most of all for two works, *Walden* – a reflection on simple living in natural surroundings, and his essay "Civil Disobedience," (originally published as "Resistance to Civil Government" – a claim in favor of disobedience to an unjust government. Both of these seminal works reflect ideas which I believe resonate profoundly with Jewish theology.

First, Thoreau's mysticism is reflective of the spiritual nature of ideas contained in the biblical book of Psalms and many other similar lyrical works – all the way forward to writings like those of Rabbi Abraham Joshua Heschel. Thoreau's choice to live in a wooded area on land owned by his friend Ralph Waldo Emerson, where he built a small, but reasonably comfortable cabin for two years and two months (July 4, 1845 to September 6, 1847), was intended to provide the ambience conducive to deep meditation.

In *Walden*, he explained his venture in this immortal description, which, in many ways, sums up his life's philosophy:

"I went to the woods because I wished to live deliberately, to front only the essential facts of life, and see if I could not learn what it had to teach, and not, when I came to die, discover that I had not lived. I did not wish to live what was not life, living is so dear; nor did I wish to practice resignation, unless it was quite necessary. I wanted to live deep and suck out all the marrow of life, to live so sturdily and Spartan-like as to put to rout all that was not life, to cut a broad swath and shave close, to drive life into a corner, and reduce it to its lowest terms, and, if it proved to be mean, why then to get the whole and genuine meanness of it, and publish its meanness to the world; or if it were sublime, to know it by experience, and be able to give a true account of it in my next excursion."

Thoreau refused to live a life without meaning. In his view, "The mass of men lead lives of quiet desperation." Henry David Thoreau lived a life filled with meaning and purpose.

In another passage, from his Journal, he wrote: "Our life is frittered away by detail. Simplify, simplify."

The transcendentalists, presided over by Emerson, believed that intuition was an inborn gift with which all humans were endowed. Thoreau had long embraced an appreciation of nature as a source of spiritual truths. The twelfth century scholar and theologian Maimonides held a similar view, that awareness of the Creator came best by appreciating the natural world which God created. Thoreau wrote in his *Journal* of a trip to Walden Pond when he was four years old, and how attracted he was to the natural world. That very young experience was for him a spiritual awakening. Thoreau's mother, Cynthia Dunbar Thoreau, related that her son would occasionally be found awake at night gazing at the heavens. He told his mother that he had been looking through the stars to see if God could be seen behind them.

Walter Harding, in his biography of Thoreau, mentioned above, writes this:

"Transcendentalists believed ...that there was a body of knowledge innate within man and that this knowledge transcended the senses. ... This knowledge was the voice of God within man – his conscience, his moral sense, his inner light, his over-soul."

This leads us to another of Thoreau's beliefs which jive with Jewish tradition; namely that justice and fairness were part of being human. In the words of Martin Luther King, Jr., who, along with many other modern human rights warriors, such as Mahatma Gandhi, believed that "the arc of the moral universe is long, but it bends toward justice."

In 1848, Thoreau delivered before the Concord Lyceum his lecture, "The Rights and Duties of the Individual in Relation to Government", published a year later as "Civil Disobedience". In the summer of 1846, Thoreau had preferred to go to jail because he refused to pay the poll tax, on the ground that the funds were used by a government of which he disapproved.

The last two years of Thoreau's life (he died in 1862) were during the Civil War, and his journals show that the evils of slavery were very much on his mind. In 1854 he delivered an angry lecture denouncing slavery. He believed, as Judaism has always taught, that "action from principle" changes individuals and society.

The Jewish theologian Martin Buber wrote from Jerusalem that he found some of Thoreau's writings very resonant, especially the idea of "Civil Disobedience". Thoreau's writings, said Buber, had authenticity for all time.

Another idea concurrent in the writings of Thoreau and found in Judaism, is the over-emphasis on materialism and consumerism. In Pirke Avot (2:7), we read "the more possessions, the more worry." In Thoreau's view, "Most of the luxuries, and many of the so-called comforts of life, are not only not indispensable, but positive hindrances to the elevation of mankind."

In *Walden,* we read that Thoreau went into a modified hibernation, to gain the attainment of an inner clarity of vision, and an appreciation of the natural world, while on the outside the world had been "bleared, smeared with trade." He proposes an ascetic life of voluntary poverty and simplicity. He saw the world as sacred (Rabbi Heschel would surely agree!) and so he began his mornings with a sacramental rite of purification, a bathing in the Walden pond, whose waters he considered to be pure and sacred. Such an act is so similar to the Jewish practice of bathing in the holy waters of the mikveh, that one wonders if he was not in some unknowable way familiar with that ancient Jewish custom. For Thoreau and for pious Jews, the idea seems to be purifying oneself of the crassness and coarseness of the world of commerce.

Students of the modern movement of environmentalism would find much in both Judaism and in the writings of Thoreau that blend very naturally.

In sum, there are multiple points of connection between the philosophy and writings of Henry David Thoreau, and of the tradition of Judaism. Both inspire the reader with awe and respect.

| 15 |

The Hebrew Prophets

The influence of the biblical Hebrew Prophets is so huge, it is almost impossible to measure.

I want to mention three examples of their influence on the world.

First, a visit to Jerusalem by the late Professor Walter Kaufmann, of Princeton University, who was a Fulbright research professor at The Hebrew University in Jerusalem in 1962-63. This happened to be the year that I spent my junior year at the Jewish Theological Seminary in Israel.

I was the chairperson of a student committee to invite guest speakers to address our twelve rabbinical students who were studying at The Hebrew University. I invited Professor Kaufmann to speak to our students, and it was a fascinating experience.

Dr. Kaufmann had published his well-known book, *The Faith of a Heretic*, the year before, and although Jewish in origin, was an avowed atheist.

During our discussion, Kaufmann expressed his deep admiration of the biblical prophets. That experience left a strong impression on me: that an atheist Jewish scholar had such a strong admiration of biblical prophets was amazing to me, and his statement never left my memory.

The second example is the philosophy of the founding father of the State of Israel, and its first Prime Minister, David Ben-Gurion.

Parenthetically, one day during my studying at The Hebrew University, I was sitting in a lecture given by Professor Kaufmann, and lo and behold, in walks Prime Minister David Ben-Gurion, with his bodyguard, who took seats on the first row.

Ben-Gurion was well-known for his intellectual appetite. His libraries in his home/museum in Tel Aviv, as well as in his home/museum in Sdeh Boker in Israel's Negev desert, are all totally book-lined.

Ben-Gurion was not a fan of post-biblical, rabbinic literature, such as the Talmud and its commentaries. It was the biblical prophets which motivated him – in his passionate quest for justice.

The third example is the strongest impression I have about the importance of the biblical Hebrew prophets. This powerful impression comes from my professor at The Jewish Theological Seminary of America, Abraham Joshua Heschel.

Professor Heschel has authored many important books, but surely one of the most important is *The Prophets.*

While the contents of this volume are extremely significant, it is the influence of writing the book on its author which is most fascinating.

Professor Heschel spent most of his life in academic scholarship. But after writing his book on the biblical prophets his life changed dramatically. The message he received from re-writing this book (the original version, in German, was his doctoral dissertation for the University of Berlin), was that book learning must lead to action, and that God cares passionately about humanity. A prophet is someone who intensely feels that divine care.

Heschel became a powerful voice in the political and social problems of the world. The issues that he fought over include civil rights for black Americans, the protest against the war in Vietnam, the rescue of Russian Jewry, and Catholic-Jewish relations. His name became strongly associated with all of these movements. He famously became a close friend and co-worker with Dr. Martin Luther King, Jr.

The Prophets

I turn now to the prophets of Israel, who lived in a relatively short period of time, from the eighth and seventh centuries. A small group of eloquent, charismatic and influential prophets has had an outsized influence on world history.

I refer to the important literary prophets such as Isaiah, Jeremiah, Amos and Hosea.

These iconic biblical figures are known for their uncompromising, individualistic proclivities. They were not concerned with the approval of society, or consequences to their physical well-being. The only force that affected them was the word of God.

The prophets were carried by a divine compulsion that gave them no peace, no rest. The only important direction that was important to them was, "Thus saith the Lord..."

The prophets were instruments of God; at times unwilling instruments (Moses, Jeremiah, Jonah), but they carried out what they thought God demanded.

"The lion hath roared, who shall not fear? The Lord God hath spoken, who shall not prophesy?"[1]

In the words of the prophet Jeremiah[2], there is this revealing passage:

You have seized me, Lord, and have enthralled me;
You have laid your hand upon me and have overpowered me.

If I say I will not make mention of Him
Nor speak anymore in His name,
His word would be like a burning fire in my heart,
Shut up in my bones,
And though I struggle to withhold it,
I cannot.

The prophets frequently criticize the social order. They aim at specific evils. They denounce kings to their faces, and openly reproach leading men. They berate mobs for idolatry.

King David watched the lovely Bathsheba bathing nude on her rooftop, and desired her. So the king sent Joab to put Uriah in front where the fiercest fighting was, and Uriah was killed. After Bathsheba mourned for her husband, David brought her to his house and she became his wife and bore him a son.[3]

"But the thing David had done displeased the Lord. And the Lord sent Nathan to David. He came to him and said, 'There were two men in the same city, one rich and one poor. The rich man had very large flocks and herds, but the poor man had only one little ewe lamb. ... One day a traveler came to the rich man, but he was loath to take

---

(1)   Amos 3:8.
(2)   Jeremiah 20:7-9.
(3)   II Samuel 11.

anything from his own flocks to prepare a meal for the guest who had come to him, so he took the poor man's lamb and prepared it for the man who had come to him.' David became furious at the man, and said to Nathan, 'As the Lord lives, the man who did this deserves to die! He shall pay for the lamb four times over, because he did such a thing and showed no pity.' And Nathan said to David, 'That man is you!'"[4]

Another story, in a similar vein, is that of Naboth's vineyard. The vineyard adjoined the King's palace, and King Ahab desired the vineyard. He offered a fair price, but Naboth refused, claiming that the vineyard was his ancestral possession. The queen, Jezebel, was a person with initiative, but no conscience. She set a trap and plotted against Naboth. She hired men to testify falsely against him, and he was charged with treason. Naboth was stoned, and Ahab took control of the vineyard. Then the word of the Lord came to the prophet Elijah the Tishbite, saying:

"Go down and confront King Ahab of Israel in Samaria. He is now in Naboth's vineyard; he has gone down there to take possession of it. Say to him, 'Thus said the Lord, Would you murder and take possession? Thus said the Lord. In the very place where the dogs lapped up Naboth's blood, the dogs will lap up your blood too.'"[5]

The words of the prophets related to the evils of society. They did not concern themselves with the temple cult alone, or "religious" matters. Their concern was a moral society, the corrupt politics of their day. The prophet was God's representative on earth, the independent supervisor of the community.

The prophet was not a fortune teller. Any predictions were conditional. "If" you continue in this path, your society will come to an end. A society that is corrupt will be punished by destruction. The prophet warned of sin, idolatry and acts of evil.

"Turn back, each of you, from your wicked ways... But

(4)   II Samuel 12.
(5)   I Kings 21:17-21.

they will say, 'It is no use. We will keep on following our own plans, each of us will act in the willfulness of his evil heart'."[6]

The prophets emphasized moral demands of God above ritual requirements. They belittled sacrificial worship, which they found to be an empty, meaningless façade. They saw no concomitant moral commitment. The masses relied on animal sacrifice and Temple worship as magic, just as many rely on the superficial performance of rituals today.

The Hebrew prophets were solitary men of God. They communed with God in the silence of the night. They were haunted by a vision that set them apart from others. They were often looked upon with disapproval, as strange people. Few understood them or appreciated them. Many hated them.

"Hosea married an adulteress by way of impressing a lesson on the minds of his people. Isaiah walked the streets of Jerusalem barefoot and naked for three years. That was his way of conveying a conviction to the lazy souls of Judah that as prisoners of Assyria, they would march into captivity completely naked.[7] Jeremiah clamped a wooden yoke around his neck and walked among his followers in awkward posture to emphasize the burden that was on his heart. The Hebrew prophets were unusual men and did highly unusual things."[8]

They circulated in crowds, at the city gates, in the Temple. We know very little of their family life. Amos tended sheep and cared for sycamore trees. Jeremiah never married.

But they were skillful preachers and poets, great orators. Their messages are unparalleled in other cultures. They weaved beautiful, moving images. They were superb pedagogues.

The prophets arose in a background of base religion. The religion of the surrounding peoples was primitive, primarily agricultural. The masses attempted to placate the gods of nature to produce a good harvest. Hebrew prophets denounced the people when they became assimilated into pagan cults. Many local gods invaded Israelite religious life. The moral standards which accompanied pagan worship were an abomination to the

(6) Jeremiah 18:11-12.
(7) See Isaiah 20:1-4.
(8) Beryl D. Cohen, The Prophets, p. 159.

Hebrew prophets. The orgiastic rituals stirred pagan worship to a frenzy, when they were maddened by dances, drinking wine, mutilated their bodies, offered their sons on the altar, and employed cult prostitutes. Sexual license was encouraged.

By contrast, Rabbi Abraham Joshua Heschel describes the ancient Hebrew prophet's "use of emotional and imaginative language, concrete in diction, rhythmical in movement, artistic in form, and marks his style as poetic. Yet it is not the sort of poetry that takes its origin, to use Wordsworth's phrase, 'from emotion recollected in tranquility.' Far from reflecting a state of inner harmony or poise, its style is charged with agitation, anguish, and a spirit of nonacceptance. The prophet's concern is not with nature, but with history, and history is devoid of poise."

"Above all, the prophets remind us of the moral state of a people: Few are guilty, but all are responsible. If we admit that the individual is in some measure conditioned or affected by the spirit of society, an individual's crime discloses society's corruption. In a community not indifferent to suffering, uncompromisingly impatient with cruelty and falsehood, continually concerned for God and every man, crime would be infrequent rather than common."[9]

"The gods are on the side of the stronger," according to Tacitus. The prophets proclaimed that the heart of God is on the side of the weaker. God's special concern is not for the mighty and the successful, but for the lowly and the downtrodden, for the stranger and the poor, for the widow and the orphan.[10]

(9) The Prophets, chapter one.
(10) The Prophets, Volume 1, p. 167.

Part III
Religion and Ritual

| 16 |

Kashrut and Kedushah

Nature has wonderfully and abundantly provided man with many means of defense against the forces of physical destruction and pain in the world. It has provided us with a shield to resist the blows of numerous forces outside our bodies. For example, the soles of our feet are thick, and hard to penetrate so that we are not hurt or harmed by stepping on rough objects. What nature has done for our bodies, it has also done for our spirits and emotions. It has given us a psychological shield, a sturdy heart, to prevent us from the adversity of life's daily blows to our psychological make-up. Since evil is such a common phenomenon in the world, we must brace ourselves against the collapse of our minds each time we learn of a tragic occurrence. We are able to take these things in our stride because of our thick emotional shield that defends the heart from the slings and arrows of misfortune.

But like other protective shields, this very means of defense must, of necessity, render us insensitive to many of the deep emotional sensations of living. As our protective shield conceals our pain, it also dulls our sensitivity to appreciate and love. While it wards off the arrows, it likewise numbs feelings of compassion, for that is its purpose – to prevent us from becoming overwhelmed by our emotions.

Thus, we face a great paradox in life. While we do not want to be destroyed each time we come face-to-face with bad news, neither do we want to be crass and callous to others. A physician has to face this dilemma more than most of us. He witnesses pain and death everyday; he wants his protective emotional shield to guard him from the trauma of witnessing human pain, yet he does not want to treat his patient as a machine or robot. What the physician faces in his profession, all of us face in our dealings with our fellow humans.[1]

This message is brought home very clearly in a scene from

---

(1)   Cf. Stephen Geller, "The Common and the Uncommon," *Conservative Judaism* 19/3, Spring, 1965: 57-62.

Thornton Wilder's play, "Our Town".[2] Emily, who has died during childbirth, is given the rare privilege by the Stage Manager to return to her home in Grover's Corners, New Hampshire, to live one day with her family. In the house she is greatly disappointed because her family seems too preoccupied with their daily chores to stop and appreciate life. Their sensitivities are dulled by the protective shields on their hearts to feel the finer sensations of life. At last Emily cries out to the Stage Manager, "I can't go on. It goes so fast. We don't have time to look at one another. ... Oh, earth, you're too wonderful for anybody to realize you." Whereupon she turns to the Stage Manager and asks: "Do any human beings ever realize life while they live it – every, every minute?" The Stage Manager answers: "No, the saints and poets, maybe – they do some."

Judaism's Answer

What is the Jewish answer to this dilemma, of not letting the protective covering of our hearts prevent us from feeling the finer sensations of living? The Stage Manager in Wilder's play formulates his answer very well, though obliquely: "The saints and poets, maybe – they do some." Somehow, if our lives are to be truly human, we have to become saints and poets. This is the role of Judaism in our lives to make us saints and poets, at least some of the time, in some aspects of life.

The word in Hebrew that best describes the way of life of a saint or poet is *kedushah* – inadequately translated as "holiness." The Jewish way of life is replete with acts of holiness.

Martin Buber has written that life may be divided into two realms – that which has been sanctified and that which is yet to be sanctified. Judaism's means of sanctifying that which is not yet sanctified are the *mitzvot* (commandments). Whenever we recite a *berakhah* (blessing) over a *mitzvah* we say: *asher kideshanu be-mitzvotav* ("who has sanctified us by His commandments"). The life of the Jew is filled with such

---

(2) Thornton Wilder, *Our Town: A Play in Three Acts,* New York: Harper and Row, 1938, 1957; <dokumen.tips/download/link/our-town-full-text.html>, Act Three.

sanctifying acts, endowing our lives with great significance,[3] filling the hours and moments of each day with opportunities to rise to the status of saint and poet.

By linking piety with poetry, I believe Wilder had deep insight into the nature of life. Only a person with musical training could appreciate the minute details of a musical score. By the same token, only a person versed in the holiness of each detail of life – of simple daily acts such as eating a piece of bread – could be sensitive to the tremendous significance of that simple act. Such a person has the sensitivity of a poet and the piety of a saint.

The word *kedushah*, or holiness, infuses the lifeblood of Jewish tradition at every turn. It appears in many grammatical forms in our liturgy and *halakhah* (Jewish law); the 18 daily *Amidah* prayers contain the *kedushah*: *kadosh, kadosh, kadosh* ("Holy, Holy, Holy [is the Lord of hosts]"); on Friday night and Sabbath morning, we recite the *kiddush*; a mourner recites the *kaddish*, the sanctification of God's name; when one marries, the *kiddushin* ceremony is performed; when we make *havdalah*, we say, *hamavdil beyn kodesh le-ḥol* ("The Holy One who separates the holy and the profane"); God is designated as *Hakadosh Barukh Hu* ("the Blessed Holy One"); when performing a pious public act, we sanctify God's name (*kiddush ha-Shem*).

These are just some of the means our ancestors have passed down to us to help us become saints and poets – at least part of the time. These are the ways in which the Jew overcomes life's dilemmas: while not becoming overwhelmed by daily crises, one can still develop a sensitivity to the beauty, poetry, piety, and sanctity of life.

The *mitzvot* of daily living are sensitizers that constantly prod us into feeling the mystery and awe of life, the wonderment and grandeur of humankind. It is the small act that counts: the washing of the hands, the recitation of a prayer, the eating of the matzah, the affixing of the mezuzah – these are the elements that add poetry and piety to a life that at times is characterized by the prosaic and the mundane. Abraham Joshua Heschel described it as follows: "in doing the finite, we can perceive the infinite."

---

(3)   Cf. Max Kadushin, *Worship and Ethic: A Study in Rabbinic Judaism*, Chapter IV: The Experience of Worship, New York: Bloch Publishing, 1963, pp. 63-66.

The Dietary Laws (*Kashrut*)

If we agree that the role of Judaism is to sanctify us and our lives, and that this must be done via the minutia of daily living, then we must stand in awe of our ancestors who saw that the most repetitive thing that one does in life is eat. Anything that sanctifies the process of consuming food must demand our attention a good part of every day of our lives.

The kitchen, dining table, and family meal are ubiquitous in our lives; if the experience of eating can be made to infuse poetry and piety in them, then we will have countless opportunities to become holy. The system of *kashrut* has one and only one purpose. It is not to keep us healthy but to keep us holy, for since the destruction of the Temple in Jerusalem, tradition tells us that the Jewish home – the repository of all Jewish values – is the sanctuary of the Jew.[4] If the Jewish home is our sanctuary, the Jewish table is our altar. Our meal is the sacrificial worship service, and all of us who eat are the priests consecrated to divine service.

Imagine the power and revolutionary implications behind this novel idea in the Bible and Talmud, that all Israel are priests, that all of us are holy people and we constitute a holy nation, that our tables are the central places of worship in our lives, and that the home is the Jewish sanctuary. The Jewish People have yet to feel full effects of the compelling force and moral cogency of this idea, even though it has been in existence for thousands of years.

Our daily meals are the vehicles that bring us to the dwellings of the poets and saints that Wilder mentioned. An ordinary person eats his daily bread, the pious person partakes of God's bounty; the ordinary person looks upon food as that part of the world provided to keep us alive, the pious person sees the act of partaking of food as one of the acts of life that can grant us the sense of infinity through prayer and ritual.[5] Through the recitation of the words of Torah at our "private sanctuary", as we are commanded to do during every meal, our table experience

(4)   B Berakhot 55A.
(5)   Abraham Joshua Heschel, *Man is Not Alone: A Philosophy of Religion*, New York: Farrar, Straus and Young, 1951, 273ff.

becomes an act of the worship of God.[6]

A Jewish custom bids us to recite: "Lift up your hands in holiness and bless the Lord,"[7] as we raise our hands and wash them before the *Ha-motzee* (the blessing over bread) and then lift the bread as we say *Ha-motzee*. In this way, we symbolically show that the act of eating will lift us up spiritually as well as physically, and by doing so we will be transformed into saints and poets – if just for the moment.[8]

The Ethical Implications of Kashrut

It is important to dispel the widely held notion that the dietary laws are an antiquated hygienic program for improving the physical care of human beings. Although some of the rules and regulations of the system of dietary laws may have at one time been connected with rules of health, this is by no means their primary purpose.

I have already indicated that we observe *kashrut* not to be healthy, but to be *holy*. Behind the laws and rules of the Jewish dietary tradition there lies a complex and deep-seated ethical basis.[9] Below are some salient examples of Jewish dietary laws:

- Judaism has developed the most humane method of slaughter known to humans – the instantaneous death of an animal through the severing of the trachea and esophagus;
- The person granted permission by the Jewish community to perform this act (the *shohet*) must be a pious Jew trained both in his sacred trade and in the Jewish laws of holiness;[10]

(6)   Pirke Avot 3:3 – "Rabbi Simeon said, When three people eat at a table and do not speak words of Torah there, it is as though they had eaten from the sacrifices of the dead."
(7)   Psalm 134:2.
(8)   Samuel Dresner, "Mitzvah: The Way of Man," *Educators Assembly Yearbook* (1965): 35. I am indebted to Rabbi Dresner's writings for many of the points made here.
(9)   Cf. Jacob Milgrom, "The Biblical Diet Laws as an Ethical System: Food and Faith," *Interpretation* 17/3, July, 1963: 288–301. I have drawn heavily on this essay.
(10)   Samuel Dresner, *The Jewish Dietary Laws,* Burning Bush Press, New York, 1966, 27ff.

- The *shohet* must use a knife that has been carefully inspected for its sharpness on both sides of the blade (in case he mistakenly uses the dull side). Since the act of killing an animal is done with great reluctance and with only the greatest religious consideration, the *shohet* must pronounce a blessing before the act of *shehitah*;
- The *shohet* has studied the laws of Judaism and knows that it is forbidden to kill an animal and its offspring on the same day – so as to avoid any possibility of an animal witnessing the pain of its young;
- To further sensitize human beings to the importance of respecting life – in animals as well as humans – the blood is completely drained from the animal before it is to be consumed;
- Jews are aware that the dietary tradition forbids them to eat a limb or body part that has been severed from a living animal – as is the custom among some Eastern tribes to this day;
- The Jew who keeps the dietary laws knows that part and parcel of the way of life he observes includes a prohibition against hunting, for animals can be killed *only* for consumption and not as a sport. For this reason, the slaughter must be done by a *shohet*. It is noteworthy that in one medieval Passover *haggadah*, the wicked son, (*rasha*) is illustrated as a hunter. We know, too, that our forefather Jacob was a tent-dweller and his brother Esau was a hunter;
- The Jew, who knows that blood is the symbol of life and for whom the eating of blood is forbidden, develops an abhorrence for food and any type of violence resulting in the flow of blood. Furthermore, any act of bloodshed precludes the Jew from eating an egg with a blood spot found in it;
- A Jew who observes the dietary laws should know that he must feed his animal before he himself sits down to a meal. This is part of the same legal system that prescribes the requirements for kosher slaughtering and kosher meat preparation;
- A vegetarian need not observe most of the dietary laws; he does not need two sets of dishes or kosher meat, nor

is there a need to wait between the consumption of meat and dairy products. According to the Book of Genesis, humans were at complete harmony with the animal kingdom in the Garden of Eden and were meant to be vegetarians. Permission to eat flesh came later, in Noah's generation, as a concession to human weakness;

- According to Maimonides, the same legal system of Judaism demands that one should eat only when hungry; one must not force oneself to satiety because of the elegance of the surroundings or the expectations of one's host; one should eat only until one fourth less than full. In this way, one distinguishes between eating as an act of an animal and eating as a means of sanctifying life and serving God's noblest purposes;

- As part of the system that dictates kindness to animals, Judaism denies us the privilege of reciting the *She-he-heyanu* blessing when putting on a new pair of leather shoes – because an animal's life had to be taken to provide the leather;

- So strong is Judaism's respect for an animal's well-being, that all the laws of the Sabbath may be broken by even the most pious rabbi in order to rescue an animal from a pit if its life is in danger.

Finally, Jewish unity – the feeling of *Klal Yisrael* – though certainly not the primary basis for *kashrut*, is a valuable by-product of keeping a kosher home. In the past, as in the present, it constitutes a bulwark against the forces of assimilation in a free society. This does not mean that Jews separate themselves from the gentiles.

The dietary laws should not prevent us from social intercourse with our non-Jewish friends and neighbors. We can invite them to our homes and, if we are careful about what we eat, we can be invited to their homes. While the dietary laws need not separate us from non-Jews, they should make us aware that there are basic differences between us.

Insofar as the dietary laws foster a feeling of family unity among the Jewish People, they enable us to survive and perpetuate an ancient and noble heritage. It would be an unspeakable loss to modern civilization if Jews and their living tradition were to disappear. If the dietary laws contribute in some measure to preserving the Jewish community and its historical memories, customs, and associations, then we have all the more reason to preserve them.

If the Jewish People are to serve as a *mamlekhet kohanim ve-goi kadosh* ("a kingdom of priests and a holy nation"), then it must survive to do so. If Jews are to be the ethical ferment in society, as our ancestors wanted us to be, then we have to be alive to act as that moral force.

Maimonides tells us[11] that the very prohibition of mixing milk and meat was devised to distinguish the ancient Israelites from the pagans, who boiled the young of a goat in its mother's milk. This prohibition is mentioned no less than three times in the Torah[12], and the rabbis derived other, ancillary laws from it, namely the prohibition of mixing *any* milk with *any* meat. Archaeologists corroborate the fact that a pre-Israelite pagan who lived in the Syrian town of Ugarit indeed had a practice of boiling a kid in its mother's milk.

Thus, when we speak of Jewish and ethnic identity, we are not referring to the most base kind of nationalistic narcissism. Rather, the dietary laws act as an aid, in addition to their ethical implications, to foster the cultural preservation and spiritual mission of the Jewish People.

Conclusion

We have cited some of the ethical bases and spiritual ramifications that uphold the custom of the Jewish dietary laws – *kashrut*. This dietary system is merely an illustration of many other areas of ritual performance that give meaning, dignity, and beauty to the daily life of the Jew. Its overall purpose is to sanctify life (*kedushah*), and raise the level of human existence to lofty heights.

Further Reading:
Dresner, Samuel H., *The Jewish Dietary Laws*, Burning Bush Press, New York, 1966.

(11)   *Guide to the Perplexed* III, 42.
(12)   Exodus 23:19, 34:36; Deut. 14:21.

Friedman, Theodore, *Letters to Jewish College Students,* Jonathan David Publishers, New York, 1965, pp. 53-57, 78-83.

Steinberg, Milton, *Basic Judaism* Harcourt, Brace and Co., New York, 1947, pp. 125-129.

| 17 |

What Do We Mean By The Word "Mitzvah"?

While the Hebrew word *"mitzvah"*[1] is one of the most important concepts in Jewish tradition, it is not easily defined.

In the Torah, the word *"mitzvah"* refers to a commandment from God. There are 613 *mitzvot*. They run the gamut from the lofty commandments to love your neighbor, to give charity to the needy, and to be honest in your business dealings on the one hand; all the way to make sure to rid one's house of all leavened food before Passover, and to wear a fringed garment with a blue thread as part of your daily wardrobe, on the other hand.

In time, the word *"mitzvah"* came to be associated more with the former category than the latter. Especially among the Yiddish-speaking Jews in the last few centuries, *"mitzvah"* came to be synonymous with "the performance of a good or a kind deed." That is part of the original meaning, but it is by no means all of it. In this essay we will look at some of the ways that the Jewish tradition developed this usage of the word *"mitzvah."* That is, we will have a brief look at how rabbis (e.g., Israel Salanter and A. J. Heschel), philosophers (Martin Buber) and mystics used the term in its sense of "performing deeds of kindness." Ultimately, we will see that the performance of good and kind deeds is at the very heart of the Jewish religion.

To take one example, a *mitzvah* in the Torah is to tell the truth. Thus, telling the truth can be seen as a *mitzvah* in both meanings – as a commandment of God and as an action with positive outcomes, an act of kindness and goodness.

In Jewish tradition, acts of kindness are definitely considered a major thrust of our tradition. Caring for the sick, the homeless, the naked, the elderly, can easily fall into both

---

(1)   Hebrew plural – *mitzvot.*

categories of the connotation and denotation of the word "*mitzvah*."

In short, Judaism is a tradition of positive actions. This Jewish ideal is expressed nicely in a statement published by the Harvard Business Review:

To LOOK is one thing.
To SEE what you look at is another.
To UNDERSTAND what you see is a third.
To LEARN from what you understand is still something else.
But to ACT on what you learn is all that really matters.

An interesting question which arises in the discussion of good deeds is whether one's intention is important. Some argue that it is the deed that counts, not the intention. Others argue that a deed is only valued if it is the result of positive thoughts.

Both of these arguments can be found in the Jewish tradition.

In another well-known Talmudic statement, we learn that doing good deeds, even without a good reason, will ultimately bring one to do good deeds for a good reason.[2]

Ralph Waldo Emerson summarized this philosophy in these simple words: "Put deeds into your creed."

Throughout the ages, some individuals and groups have accused Judaism of making too many "action" demands, such as circumcision, Sabbath observance, dietary laws, etc. When Christianity was born some two thousand years ago, the attraction was the argument that God only desires love, not law, faith rather than rituals. Most modern Christian theologians agree that Judaism is as much a religion of love as it is a religion of law. Often it is the obligations of laws that bring people to actions of love.

In Jewish tradition, when one follows the Jewish way of ritual and ethical acts, one will bring much love in its wake. By following the *halakhah*, Jewish Law, one gets into the habit of helping others and doing it for positive reasons.

By helping another through acts of kindness, one can come to love the other.

---

(2)   Tractate Pesahim 50B.

The journalist Bill Moyers[3] once wrote "The sickness of our society is not that we have problems. The sickness is this ominous sense of impotence which renders us unable to act on our beliefs."

There are many stories of acts of kindness performed by well-known rabbis, so let me share one:

Rabbi Yisrael Salanter[4] was missing from his synagogue one Kol Nidre eve, the holiest night of the Jewish year. The Elders went searching for him, and they found him feeding a sick child.

"Rabbi," the students asked him, "why are you not in synagogue on this holy evening?"

"I am praying," he answered. "Every act of kindness is a prayer – a prayer that walks, moves, breathes and lives."

When Rabbi Abraham Joshua Heschel marched in Selma with Dr. Martin Luther King, Jr., to promote the civil rights of African Americans, he said something similar. "My legs are praying."

Philosopher Martin Buber[5] once taught that a single *mitzvah* is like a garment of God. Every time you perform a good deed you metaphorically grab on to that garment and you have all of God. You have grasped the basic purpose of life, the highest, personal fulfillment of life.

In doing *mitzvot* we fulfill our God-given potential, we bring out the best in ourselves and others.

Many synagogues have created a corps of people who are dedicated to the performance of *mitzvot*. People in such a group fulfill the words of the liturgy, the prayer that follows the chanting of the Haftarah, "that God bless those who provide food for visitors and charity for the poor, and all who faithfully occupy themselves with the needs of the community... May God send blessing and success to all the work of their hands, together with all Israel."

(3)   b. 1934.
(4)   1809-1883, Lithuania.
(5)   1878-1965, Austria and Jerusalem.

In Jewish mysticism it is taught that every good deed becomes a part of a spiritual garment for our soul in Paradise. The more *mitzvot* we perform here on earth, the more decorative and beautiful our garment will be in Gan Eden.

The final words of the biblical book of Kohelet (12:13) are a good way to bring our study of the *mitzvah* to a conclusion:

"The end of the matter; when all is said and done. Revere God and keep God's commandments (*mitzvot*), for this is the whole duty of man."

| 18 |

Why I Love Shabbat

So much has been written on the subject of Shabbat, the Sabbath, by many leading scholars, philosophers and educators (including my own book, *A Shabbat Reader: Universe of Cosmic Joy),* why include another essay on the Shabbat in this collection?

The answer is that since this book contains my own philosophy of Judaism, I would be remiss to omit my thoughts about my most favorite topic in Jewish life.

My teacher at the Jewish Theological Seminary, Rabbi Abraham Joshua Heschel, called the Sabbath a "palace in time." In my teaching, I frequently retell the following question asked by Rabbi Heschel:

> Since God created so much beauty in the world –
> mountains, oceans, trees, birds, rainbows, etc., why
> did God not create a beautiful sanctuary?

His reply was that God did in fact create a most exquisite sanctuary. But the sanctuary created by God is not a sanctuary in space, it is a sanctuary in time: the Sabbath.

In her eloquent book *The Sabbath World,* Judith Shulevitz calls the Sabbath "a different order of time." What an exquisite way to describe the Sabbath!

Anyone who observes the Sabbath in a strict halakhic way, or in their own personal way, will testify that this special day of the week is an extraordinary gift given by the Jewish People to the world.

Long before I changed my life from an assimilated American Jew to a Sabbath-observer, I recognized in subconscious and conscious ways that Shabbat was an event *sui generis* in the scope of one's life.

Partly it was the enchanting music of the traditional synagogues I occasionally attended. Partly it was the experience of some ineffable sensation that smothered me with an invisible spiritual blanket.

Partly it was a sensation that is indescribable, precious, and indispensable.

The ancient rabbis taught that whoever observes the Sabbath will experience a taste of Heaven.

A medieval tale relates that when God was about to give the Torah to Israel, the Almighty summoned the people and said: "My children, I have something precious that I would like to give you for all time, if you will accept My Torah and observe My commandments."

The people asked: "Master of the universe, what is the precious gift You have for us?"

The Blessed Holy One replied: "It is the world-to-come."

The people of Israel answered: "Show us a sample of the world-to-come!"

The Blessed Holy One said: "The Sabbath is a sample of the world-to-come, for that world will be one long Sabbath."[1]

Rabbi Irving (Yitz) Greenberg wrote that "According to classical Judaism, ethics is the way to serve God, ritual is the way to connect to God. Shabbat unifies the two aspects in one experience."

When I was a counselor and division head at Camp Ramah in the Pocono mountains, in the 1950s, Shabbat was so special that campers and staff alike expressed the desire to observe Shabbat in their home setting just as we did at camp. It included the wearing of white clothing, a spiritual quiet surrounding us in every corner, and the music of Jewish living hummed throughout our meals, our prayer, and our study.

Particularly meaningful was the Friday night outdoor worship, overlooking the tree-lined Pocono mountains surrounding our prayer space, inviting the Sabbath guest with the uplifting poem of Hayyim Nahman Bialik, "The Sabbath Queen."

The sun o'er the treetops no longer is seen; Come, let us go forth and greet Sabbath the Queen. Behold her descending, the holy and blest, And with her the angels of peace and of rest. Welcome, welcome, queen and bride,

(1)   Otiyot d'Rabbi Akiva.

Welcome, welcome, queen and bride. Peace be unto you, angels of peace.

One of the many touching scenes in the film, *Fiddler on the Roof*, is when all the women in the *shtetl* of Anatevka light their Shabbat candles.

Shabbat candle-lighting is a magical moment that brings Shabbat into one's home. When the women circle their arms in the air and mystically draw into the household the special aura of Shabbat, the entire ambience is transformed. Countless women, even some who do not observe Shabbat for a full day, report that lighting Shabbat candles is an incandescent moment that fills their heart and soul with an extra measure of spirituality.

The Talmudic Rabbi Shimon ben Lakish taught that "The Blessed Holy One lends us an extra soul on the eve of the Sabbath, and withdraws it at the close of the Sabbath."[2]

The holy moment of candle-lighting is the beginning of the embodiment of that extra soul.

Rabbi Jules Harlow wrote this inspirational prayer for the moment of candle lighting:

"May the light of these candles help inspire us to love You with all our hearts. May their warmth and glow radiate kindness, harmony, and joy among the members of my family; may love and devotion bind us closer to one another and to you. Amen!"

Hannah Senesh (1921–1944) was a young poet and a Special Operations Executive (SOE) member. She was one of 37 Jewish SOE recruits from Mandate Palestine who parachuted by the British into Yugoslavia during the Second World War to assist anti-Nazi forces and ultimately for the rescue of Hungarian Jews about to be deported to the German death camp at Auschwitz. She wrote several beautiful poems which are still popular today.

---

(2) Talmud, Tractate Betza 16A.

In her poem "Blessed Is the Match," she wrote this:

*Blessed is the Match
That kindles the Sabbath lights.
Blessed is The Home
That reflects the glow of the
Sabbath candles.
Blessed is The Heart
That radiates the warmth of
Sabbath peace.*

Hannah Senesh.

When I was a congregational rabbi, before retirement, the theme of Shabbat was something I spoke about at every opportunity – from the pulpit, in the classroom, and in private conversations. This was for two reasons. First because I find Shabbat to be one of the most important spiritual experiences in my entire life. Second, because I believe that the key to promoting deep Jewish living can be the observance of Shabbat. I have seen many individuals who were not connected to their Jewishness, and who started to keep Shabbat, later they continued to increase their connection to the Jewish way of life and to the Jewish People.

The well-known philosopher, Ahad Ha'am[3] wrote famously that "more than the Jewish People kept Shabbat, Shabbat kept the Jewish People." In other words, the experience of Shabbat has been, throughout the centuries, a major building block in the survival of Judaism and the Jewish People.[4]

A wonderful example of how important Shabbat has been in the steadfastness of our people, and in the spiritual power that Shabbat has provided for our people throughout the centuries is a story told by the national poet of the Jewish People, Hayyim Nahman Bialik, whom we've mentioned in other essays.

Bialik's family was cruelly deported from their home in

(3)　1856-1927, Ukraine and Tel Aviv.
(4)　See the essay in this book on Ahad Ha'am.

a village in Czarist Russia. The family found itself desolately and aimlessly wandering in a forest. Bialik's mother realized that it was Friday afternoon, and as sunset approached, she took out two little candles, kindled them, covered her face to recite the blessing over the Sabbath, and all at once the family felt as if they were home again. Between the stars sparkling in the heavens, and the Shabbat candles flickering below, they no longer felt uprooted and ashamed. The Bialik family, for a short while, felt as though they were in a peaceful, serene home.

My prayer is that more people will find in experiencing Shabbat the beauty, serenity, tranquility, and wholesomeness of God's great gift of Shabbat.

| 19 |

The Need For Hasidism in Today's World

"**N**o renewal of Judaism is possible that does not bear in itself the elements of Hasidism."[1]

Martin Buber was one of the leading proponents of incorporating components of the Hasidic Movement into modern expressions of Jewish life. Several of Buber's books deal with various aspects of Hasidism, and he is well known for his two-volume collection of Hasidic stories, which he collected and edited.[2]

Martin Buber.

The Hasidic Movement was founded by Rabbi Yisrael ben Eliezer, known popularly by the acronym the BESHT[3]. The BESHT was a Jewish mystic and healer who attracted many followers to his spiritual interpretations of Jewish liturgy and concepts.

Let's examine some of the ideas of eighteenth and nineteenth century Hasidism, its time of great flourishing.

First the BESHT emphasized joy and spontaneity in both worship and learning.

So much of the experiences of prayer and study in Eastern European Jewish life was dry and routine. Jews in Poland, Russia, and Ukraine had been persecuted and driven to live in ghettos so that their religious life centered on casuistry in learning, and rote repetition in daily prayer. Their focus was turned inward as they avoided the travails of the gentile world outside, which was so often antisemitic and smothering.

(1) From *The Legend of the Baal Shem* by Martin Buber 1878-1965, Austria and Jerusalem.
(2) *Tales of the Hasidim.*
(3) **B**aal **Sh**em **T**ov, 1700-1760.

The BESHT found ways to enliven, brighten and invigorate many aspects of Jewish life. He introduced wordless melodies (*niggunim*) into worship, which became a central part of Hasidic prayer. Dancing also gave worship a cheerful tone. The addition of telling spiritual stories also gave Jewish life a quality of lively renewal.

Spiritual interpretations of biblical texts enabled Hasidic students an opportunity to read the ancient sacred texts in a new light.

Rabbi Pesach Pruskin,[4] for example, interpreted this biblical verse:[5] "Put off your shoes from off your feet" to imply that "one must put off the habitual which encloses your feet, and you will know that the place where you are now standing is holy ground. For there is no rung of human life on which we cannot find the holiness of God everywhere and at all times."

In other words, every minute is new, fresh and an exciting experience of life. Each time one recites the prayer before eating bread (the "*motzee*"), donning a tallit, or reciting the Shema, it can be as if you never said it before in your life.

Rabbi Pruskin was teaching his followers that every experience can be holy, and can bring one closer to God. This Hasidic teaching was central to its teachers and followers, that one should find opportunities to cling to God (in Hebrew "*devekut*") at all times.

Because the Hasidic Movement emphasized closeness to God, the Hasidic masters felt that all parts of a person can be holy. Therefore, the generally accepted dichotomy between sacred and profane, religious and secular, physical and spiritual, were false dichotomies.

In the first Gospel of Matthew, it says: "Render unto Caesar what is Caesar's and to God the things that are God's."[6] In Hasidism there is no such division.

Rabbi Menahem Mendel of Kotzk[7] interpreted the biblical verse[8] "You shall be holy unto Me" to mean that one should be

---

(4)   1879-1939 Kobryn, Belarus.
(5)   Exodus 3:5.
(6)   Matthew 22:21.
(7)   1787-1859, Poland.
(8)   Leviticus 19:2.

humanly holy unto God. One should stop reaching for Heaven, and bring Heaven into our daily lives. One should hallow the everyday.

As Martin Buber expressed this thought, "All life is divided into two parts, that which is holy and that which is yet to be made holy."

Rabbi Pinhas Shapiro of Koretz[9] taught that "whoever says that the words of the Torah are one thing, and the words of the world another, must be regarded as one who denies God."

Another important idea held by the Hasidic Movement is that the rabbis encourage deep love for all living creatures as unique and precious beings. Many Hasidic teachers encourage their followers to love even their enemies.

One Hasidic teacher gave the following interpretation about the kashrut of the stork. The stork is not kosher for eating. In Hebrew, the stork is called "*Hasidah*," which means loving. If the stork is a loving animal, why then is it not considered kosher to eat? The Hasidic answer is that while the stork is loving and kind, it loves only its own kind, not strangers. In Hasidic doctrine, a kosher Jew must love the stranger, regardless of color, ethnicity, religion, etc.

Another important doctrine of Hasidism is that the life of the senses is not denied, but rather valued.

The ideal for a Hasid, as it is for Judaism in general, is not chastity, but marriage, which is the highest form of living. Hasidim relish drinking, eating, celebrating – within reasonable limits. To them, physical pleasures are the means of sanctifying life.

A Hasidic rabbi taught that one who harbors an evil urge is at a great advantage. For he can serve God with it. He can gather all his passion and warmth and pour them into the service of God. What counts is to restrain the blaze in the hour of desire and let it flow into the hours of prayer and service to God and other people.

The Midrash teaches, they remind us, that one must love God with both the good inclination ("*yetzer hatov*") as well as with the evil urge ("*yetzer hara*"). Without the *yetzer hara,* no one would raise a family, build a house, or start a business.[10]

(9)   1726-1791, Belarus and Ukraine.
(10)   Genesis Rabba 9:7.

One of the best books (of which there are so many[11]) is *Everyday Miracles: The Healing Wisdom of Hasidic Stories* by Howard W. Polsky and Yaella Wozner.

They write this about the four main functions of Hasidic stories:

- To be a bridge from past to present to uphold tradition.
- To bind Hasidism and their rabbis through emotional support.
- To reinforce the core values of Hasidism that comprise the function of its philosophy.
- To be a source of entertainment, fun, humor, and mental gymnastics.

The authors explain that Hasidic stories are "a generative invention by which the rabbis counseled their followers about specific, concrete, everyday problems, and simultaneously inculcated the core values of Hasidism. This was, indeed, a brilliant idea. There is not a single Hasidic story which does not have at its core ... a definite set of values which is more or less emphasized in guiding a supplicant to work out his problems."

Finally, Hasidic doctrine re-emphasizes a traditional Jewish idea of the importance of community. An important scholar of Hasidism, Maurice Friedman (1921-2012), formerly professor of philosophy at San Diego State University, wrote "The Hasidism of the BESHT may point to a true covenant community which does not now exist." While Jewish tradition has for millennia encouraged the formation of community in worship, celebration, and study, for the Hasidim it rose to a higher level of importance.

While several of the ideas we listed above have some background in Jewish life, for the Hasidic Movement these ideas found a more central place in worship, study, and daily Jewish living. Contemporary Judaism would gain immeasurably if these elements of Hasidic doctrine would find a stronger emphasis and a more robust emphasis in the daily life of Jews worldwide.

(11) See also *The Founder of Hasidism: Wisdom and Tales of the Baal Shem Tov* by Simcha Raz and translated by Dov Peretz Elkins.

| 20 |

Why I Love Hearing the Sound of the Shofar

Whenever I visited people in the hospital during the days between Rosh Hashanah and Yom Kippur, the most common request I received was, "Would you please blow the shofar for me. I miss that more than anything on the High Holidays, now when I'm in the hospital."

Blowing the shofar is the oldest, most colorful, best-known ritual of the High Holidays, perhaps even through the entire Jewish calendar.

Even so, the Torah does not mention the word shofar, or the name Rosh Hashanah. Using the shofar to fulfill the biblical command[1] to make the first day of the seventh month a "*Yom Teruah*" (Day of Sounding) is a rabbinic (Talmudic) tradition.

The original shofar was a simple musical instrument. It is probably the oldest musical instrument in all cultures still in use. It is created by boring a narrow passage through an animal's horn. For traditional

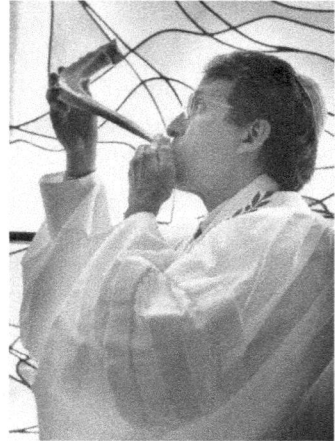

Rabbi Dov Peretz Elkins blowing the shofar.

synagogues it is the only musical instrument ever used in worship. Ironically, using instrumental music is considered "Christian," when in biblical days the use of instrumental music was a vital part of worship.[2] After the destruction of the Temple in Jerusalem, by the Romans in 70 C.E., the rabbis placed a ban on using such musical instruments as a sign of

---

(1) Numbers 29:1.
(2) See Psalm 150.

mourning for Temple days.

The Bible records several instances of shofar blowing on various special occasions. In ancient Israel the shofar was blown to signal the advent of the Jubilee Year (Leviticus 25:9), during Joshua's siege of Jericho (Joshua 6:8), when Gideon routed the Midianites (Judges 7:16), and when peace was announced (II Samuel 2:28). The shofar is also blown in several places in the Bible as a warning of danger (Nehemiah 4:14). It was sounded to proclaim a new Israelite king (I Kings 1:34).

Some Meanings of the Shofar Blasts

Below are listed several interpretations of the shofar blasts.

In popular folk literature, sounds were used to repel evil powers. Note the similarity of the shofar sounds on Rosh Hashanah and the noisemaking during the advent of the secular new year.

- A call to God to hear our prayers.
- To remind God and ourselves of the merit of our forefathers – such as Abraham during the Akedah when a ram replaced Isaac as a sacrifice.
- As a reminder of great moments of past Jewish history, such as at the giving of the Ten Commandments at Mt. Sinai[3], and the hope for a future Messianic age: "And in that day a great shofar will sound." Those who were perishing in Assyria and those who were exiled in Egypt will come and worship God on the holy mountain in Jerusalem.[4]
- The shape of the shofar is curved and bent, to symbolize a humble frame of mind.
- A reminder of the sounding of the shofar at important moments in the history of the State of Israel, such as the birth of the State on May 14, 1948.
- And most recently during the Six Day War when the holy city of Jerusalem was unified and Rabbi (Chaplain) Shlomo Goren blew the shofar at the Western Wall on June 7, 1967.

(3)   Exodus 19:19.
(4)   Isaiah 27:13.

A final interpretation is by the distinguished scholar of Jewish mysticism, Rabbi Arthur Green:[5]

The sounding of the shofar is considered an act of great mystery. The wordless but wailing shofar sounds are taken to be a "higher" or deeper expression of Israel's outcry than words can express. While the liturgy of Rosh Hashanah is perhaps the most eloquent and poetic of the year, the raw emotion of the season ("Thank You for bringing us alive to this time! Give us another year of life!") is so elemental and primitive that it is better expressed by these unrefined cries of the horn than by words of great poets.

The mystics attributed great significance to the order of the shofar blasts. One such *kavvanah,* attributed to Rabbi Isaiah Horowitz (who lived in Prague and Jerusalem in the seventeenth century), notes that each group of sounds begins with a *teki'ah,* a whole note, proceeds to *shevarim,* a "broken" note, divided into three parts, or even to *teru'ah,* an entirely fragmented sound, at least seven very brief sounds. But each broken note is followed by a whole note, another *teki'ah.* This, he says, is the message of Rosh Hashanah: "I started off whole, I became broken, even splintered into fragments, but I shall become whole again! I shall become whole again!"[6]

---

(5) From *Rosh Hashanah Readings*, ed. Dov Peretz Elkins.
(6) Many more explanations can be found in *Rosh Hashanah Readings*, pp. 163-187, Dov Peretz Elkins editor, Jewish Lights Publishing.

www.ingramcontent.com/pod-product-compliance
Lightning Source LLC
Chambersburg PA
CBHW021112090426
42738CB00006B/605